KEEPING IN TOUCH

KEEPING IN TOUCH
WRITING CLEARLY

Susan Day
Illinois State University

Elizabeth McMahan
Illinois State University

Robert Funk
Eastern Illinois University

Macmillan Publishing Company
New York

Macmillan Publishing Company
866 Third Avenue, New York, New York 10022

Library of Congress Cataloging-in-Publication Data

Day, Susan.
    Keeping in touch.

    1. English language—Rhetoric.   2. College readers.
I. McMahan, Elizabeth.   II. Funk, Robert.   III. Title.
PE1408.D37   1987   808′.0427   86-19968
ISBN 0-02-327910-9

Printing: 1 2 3 4 5 6 7   Year: 7 8 9 0 1 2 3

ISBN   0-02-327910-9

To our friend Sue LeSeure

PREFACE

In this book, we have assumed that we, the authors, and you, the teacher, share certain ideas about how composition is best taught. Some of these ideas are

- Every student must have the opportunity to write whole, meaningful essays, not just do drills.
- Each of your students has individual problems and strengths; each needs individualized assignments.
- If you had to make up and evaluate individualized assignments for each of your students, the rest of your life would be exceptionally, even desperately, bleak.

We have tried to find a compromise between the ideals of the first and second principles and the reality of the third. We'd like to see you do the best for your students and still lead a full life.

The compromise offered by the system in our book involves week-by-week units. The first activity of each unit is the key essay, which all students write. Sometimes based on readings, sometimes on discussions and short examples, these assignments are varied and lively, incrementally incorporating more and more sophisticated skills. The assignments are based on our own, our students', and our colleagues' favorites.

Before the key essays are submitted to you, they will be submitted to other members of the class. Each student then exchanges with another and writes the answers to a series of questions specifically related to the goals of the key essay. Students read and integrate the peer responses into their key essays. Then you take up both the essays and written responses.

After each key essay assignment appear three sets of follow-up exercises: A, B, and C. Each student will do items from these sets according to the strengths and weaknesses you see in each key essay. We have tried to divide the main problems we see in our students' writing into three categories:

1. Set A attempts to help the student who has fluency problems, who needs to learn to generate material and support.

2. Set B is designed for the student who is behind in traditional correctness—punctuation, sentence boundaries, and mechanics.
3. Set C will help the student who has difficulty with logical development and arrangement of ideas.

Of course, it's impossible to separate these categories completely; the categories merely give you a guideline for making your individual assignments. Every set does include more actual writing, not just filling in blanks or dotting in periods.

Becoming acquainted with the three sets of exercises before you read the key essays will, we hope, let you easily choose a set or a combination for each student. How much and what kind of evaluation to give these assignments are up to you.

The *Instructor's Manual* will provide suggestions for varying and tailoring the book's pattern to suit your schedule and teaching style. It will also give you guidelines to help you decide which exercises to assign.

This book is not as rule- and explanation-ridden as most of its kind. We rely on students' intuitive grasp of the language and on their ability to induce and deduce when given good examples and a bit of guidance. Memorization of written rules is a weak tool in comparison with discovery—which is much more fun. So, enough explanation: go on to discover *Keeping in Touch*.

For everything they've done from making the coffee to taming the computer printer, we thank our friends Sue LeSeure, Chris Maier, Laurie Haag, Laurie Dahlberg, Michele Finley, Mark Silverstein, Dan LeSeure, Dave Nelson, and Bill Weber. We're most grateful to our wonderful students at Illinois State University and Eastern Illinois University who test drove the exercises. We've also benefitted from the helpful responses of our reviewers Henry Castillo of Temple Junior College, Eric P. Hibbison of J. Sargeant Reynolds Community College, Edward C. Nolte of Norfolk State University, Beatrice B. Tignor of Prince George's Community College, and Mary E. McGann of Rhode Island College. Credit for the smooth and intelligent editing goes to Tony English and Jennifer Crewe at Macmillan Publishing.

Susan Day
Elizabeth McMahan
Robert Funk

How to Use This Text

This book, which is intended to help you improve your writing, offers individualized instruction plus plenty of writing practice. Since the design of each chapter is essentially the same, you should (after we have explained the plan) be able to proceed easily through the text with guidance from your instructor and help from your classmates and be well on your way to becoming a confident and competent writer.

As you can see from the table of contents, the book consists of fifteen chapters, each of which presents a series of assignments to take you through one week's work.

You will begin each week by writing what we call a "key essay." This assignment is often based on a short reading and involves various kinds of writing. The first assignments will be fairly easy, but they will become more challenging as you gain skill and confidence. You may also find a number of unfamiliar words in this text. Some are considered in vocabulary exercises. The others you should look up in a good, desk-sized dictionary—a writer's most valuable tool.

After you complete each key essay, you will exchange papers with a fellow student. Each of you will read the other's work. Your purpose in these "peer revision" sessions will be to help your partner improve his or her essay, but the rewards are twofold. Your partner gains the benefit of your useful suggestions while you gain experience as an editor and reviser. No skill is more essential to good writing than the ability to see when something goes wrong—or very right—with a piece of writing. You will also receive help both from your instructor and from this text in perfecting these revising skills.

After your instructor has read your key essay, she or he will decide which of the three sets of exercises in each chapter will best provide the practice you need. You will be assigned activities to help you overcome some weakness or to reinforce strengths in your writing. Although these exercises sometimes involve drills to eliminate errors in punctuation or grammar, you'll not get stuck with such tiresome chores every week. Often your exercises will involve further writing practice and will encourage you to be imaginative and creative.

Thus, with relatively little mental strain, you will find yourself discovering new ways to invent interesting things to say as well as improving your ability to write down these ideas clearly, logically, and correctly.

Susan Day
Elizabeth McMahan
Robert Funk

CONTENTS

1

FIRST IMPRESSIONS: A TWO-PARAGRAPH ESSAY

In your first essay you'll be writing a description of yourself and trading descriptions with your classmates. The directions for writing your essay follow.

Good — Writing Sample

KEY ESSAY

Sample

Toes

Your first paragraph should include two things:

1. A detailed description of what you are wearing today.
2. Your ideas about what your appearance today would suggest to a stranger.

In this paragraph, be as specific as you can. Blue jeans aren't just blue jeans: the ones you are wearing have something distinctive about them. Are the knees worn and dirty, or is the denim crisp and clean? Do they smell like fabric softener, engine oil, or yesterday's lunch?

As you think about your description, try to look at yourself as strangers—perhaps the other students in your class—see you today. Do you give the impression of being shy or outgoing? Lighthearted or serious? Well-off or poverty-stricken? Would someone guess that you worked in an office or on a construction crew? Tell what details of your description would inspire the guesses that other people might make about you.

In the second paragraph tell whether what others might think is correct or not. For example, you could say, "My designer jeans may give people the idea that I'm rich, but actually I got them out of the ragbag at the Goodwill thrift shop." Or you might write, "My sloppy and careless attire contrasts with the orderliness of my mind," or "My clean, neat appearance reflects my careful, conservative attitudes." Each sentence like this should have an example or more details to go with it: "My sloppy and careless attire contrasts with the orderliness of my mind. For instance, this is the first day of class, and I have already bought the texts for all my courses, planned my routes from building to building on the campus map (which I sent for in advance), and set up a reasonable weekly study schedule."

Try to fill at least one side of a page with your two paragraphs.

QUESTIONS FOR ANALYZING WRITING

After your class has finished writing, exchange essays with someone else. Read your partner's essay, and then write sentences answering the following questions:

1. How many sentences did your partner write in paragraph one? How many sentences are in paragraph two?
2. What are five details that the writer used in the description?
3. What is one impression that the writer thinks he or she might give others today?
4. Does the writer think that this impression is correct or not? Why?

After you answer those questions, write a question for your partner. This question doesn't have to be of any special type or form. Any question that you think of when you read the essay will do: "Are there many great bargains at the thrift shop?" for example, or "Do you ever fall off your green platform shoes?" or "Can you give some advice about how to be more orderly?" Give your answers and your question to your partner. Your partner's responses to your writing may make you want to clarify your essay before you turn it in.

EXERCISES

SET A: WRITING FLUENTLY

1. Write an answer to the question your partner wrote for you. If the question is too embarrassing (you really would rather not describe your platform shoe injuries) or offensive ("Who did *that* to your hair?"), make up a question you would prefer and answer that. Make your answer as specific as you can.

Wed -
Freewriting

2. Collect a pen, some paper, and a friend or alarm to time you, and settle yourself in a familiar place (your room, a school lounge, a favorite hangout). Begin your writing by describing the sounds you hear, and go on from there. You may find yourself launched into thoughts inspired by the sounds, or you may just continue to find more and more sounds to write about as you concentrate. Keep writing for five minutes.

This is a *free writing* exercise. In free writing you must write continuously; even if you can't think of anything to say, you must keep writing "I can't think of anything" or repeat what you last wrote until something finally comes to you (and it will). This practice seems difficult, but what makes it easier is that you don't have to worry at all about punctuation, logic, sentence structure, spelling, or any of those things that tend to get your flow of thought blocked up.

Remember, you must not stop. After five minutes of free writing at your familiar place, relax, shake out your writer's cramp, and do five more minutes of free writing. That's enough for one day.

There are several explanations (some of them really boring) of why free writing is good for you. The simplest reason is that it gives you a chance to let your thoughts flow from your mind to your page without the interference of worries about following the right rules. You may never have had a chance to do that before, and you need to achieve this flow if you're going to write well. After all, you can't revise, edit, and beautify a page with nothing on it.

3. Now we're going to send you to an *unfamiliar* place to do some writing. Find some place you don't know very well (a restaurant, a swimming hole, a video arcade, a seamy cocktail lounge), and spend a few minutes observing your surroundings and the people there. Then write twenty-five questions about it. You'll have to jump-start your imagination along about number fifteen: "Why did the landlord think that this color of green was acceptable?"

"What are those funny vegetables?" "How am I going to get rid of this pushy lout?"

Writing questions about a subject, even forcing yourself to write them, is a useful way to develop your thinking. When you get past the questions that are easy to write, you begin to look beyond the obvious and superficial level. We will continue to encourage you to use this technique as you work on your essays.

SET B: WRITING ACCURATELY

1. The following sentences include sets of blanks for you to fill in with appropriate words or phrases. Check your dictionary to make sure the words you fill in are spelled correctly. Copy the whole sentence with your additions, paying attention to the placement of the commas.

a. My best character qualities are _____, _____, and _____.
b. _____, _____, and _____ are little habits people have that drive me crazy. (Note: Use an *-ing* word like *cursing* in each blank.)
c. I have always wanted to _____, to _____, and to _____.
d. Three major improvements I would like to see in my hometown are _____, _____, and _____.
e. Romantic films have the power to _____, _____, and _____ me.

2. Combine each group of sentences into one sentence. We'll do the first one for you.

a. You may like to travel.
   You may be interested in traveling alone.
   You are a woman.
   I have some tips for you.

One possible combination: If you are a woman who likes travel and is interested in traveling alone, I have some tips for you.

b. My friend is a woman.
   She travels alone a lot.
   She has given me some good advice.
   The advice is about traveling alone.
c. You may be on a train or plane.
   You choose your departure and arrival times.

Check the time of your arrival at your destination.
Be sure your arrival will be during daylight hours.
d. The station or airport may be far from your hotel.
You will need to find out the best way to get to your hotel.
Taxis are expensive.
e. You have more options during the day.
A long walk is a good way to see a city.
You may be able to catch a bus.
Some hotels run shuttle buses during the day.

3. In the following paragraph Peg Bracken describes her grandparents' hometown, using specific details and remarks to give a general idea of what the place was like.

> Ganister was a town of frame houses: white ones, brown ones, green ones, usually two-storied and front-porched. If there were brick houses, I wasn't aware of it. I think any available bricks went into the streets and the sidewalks, where green moss grew quietly between them, and my father said that what you did in Ganister on Saturday nights was listen to it grow. He would sometimes add that in the hot humid daytimes, you could also watch the labels slide off the catsup bottles. Like many men, he was dutiful about visits to the in-laws, though not overly enthusiastic.
>
> —*From "Of Copper Bowls and Kansas" in* A Window Over the Sink, *copyright © 1981 by Peg Bracken. Reprinted by permission of Harcourt Brace Jovanovich, Inc.*

Go back over the paragraph in order to answer the following questions:

● How many sentences are in the paragraph?
● How many sentences can you make out of the information in Bracken's first sentence? (In other words, identify a list of short sentences like those in exercise 2, Set B of this chapter.) Write them out.
● How many commas are in the paragraph?
● How many details and examples does the writer include?
● What general statement could you make about the town described?

Now, write a paragraph of similar length and style about your own hometown or another town you know well. The content may be quite different (if, for example, you're from Chicago, Birmingham, or Moscow), but try to pattern it the same way Peg Bracken does, using details and comments to get across an impression of the place.

SET C: WRITING LOGICALLY AND COHERENTLY

1. We have written a paragraph that stays pretty much at a general level. It's badly in need of details to develop it, clarify it, and make it more interesting. You must provide these. Be as creative as you wish; feel free to alter the wording of our sentences; use first person (I) if that works best. Try to expand the 69-word paragraph to 200 words or more.

> A first date is always a risky occasion, with endless possibilities for disaster and disappointment. Sometimes both people realize at the very beginning of the date that it is a mistake. At other times they get to know each other a little before they see that their interests and personalities don't fit well at all. And frequently, only at the end of the date does the mismatch become clear.

2. Following is a description of the kind of work done by a Belgian company, owned by Duchatelet, that customizes new cars. It contains an impressive list of details.

> Starting with a Mercedes fully equipped with the conventional luxury options, Duchatelet adds such amenities as a walnut-veneer, leather-trimmed, fully contoured dashboard; a walnut cocktail cabinet fitted into the dashboard with silver beakers and a Cartier lighter; thermic, sunray-filtering curtains on the windows in the rear compartment; console equipment including an automatic-reverse cassette player, a stereo with an amplifier, sound equalizer and panoramic control; a central console between the front seats that houses a refrigerator; and armrests that form a walnut table for glasses, goblets and a Cartier clock. Additional options include a telephone and television set.

> —*Paul Frere, "Carat by Duchatelet,"* Road and Track
> *(Sept. 1985), p. 106.*

Just counting those specifics is a bit staggering, but do it anyway. We don't know what some of that stuff *is*, but we sure get the general idea.

Write a paragraph of about the same length using the same organization that Frere does: a listing of details. Describe a car, motorcycle, boat, or bicycle that you have known well, being as specific as you can. Your development may run more toward enumeration of the rust holes in the hood than to Cartier accessories, but you can still leave a vivid impression. If you string all the details in a row as Frere does, be sure to notice and imitate his punctuation. (He uses semicolons to separate lists of lists.)

Describing a place

3. In your key essay you described your appearance and did some analysis of it. Now write a similar essay about a place. Write a list of places that are special to you for one reason or another. Your essay will probably turn out better if you choose specific places (a childhood hideaway, a certain waterfall) rather than general ones (Hawaii, outer space). To decide which place to choose for your essay, take a piece of scratch paper and write the details you could use for three of the choices that look promising. You should soon see which choice will allow you to provide the freshest, most plentiful details.

In the first paragraph of your essay identify the place and describe it in detail. In the second paragraph of the essay explain why it is special to you. Did something important happen to you there? Do you associate it with certain good feelings (peace, excitement, challenge, victory)? Or does it just seem to suit you down to the ground? If so, why? Each paragraph should be over 100 words long, but the two don't have to be equal in length.

CHAPTER SUMMARY

In this chapter you've studied

- using details in a description
- helping other students analyze writing
- free writing for ideas and detailed development
- writing questions about a subject
- using commas in a parallel series
- combining sentences for smoothness

2

AT WORK: USING EXAMPLES

The article we reprint here is about qualities that may be necessary in a successful executive. After you read the article, we'll ask you to reflect on your own work and what it takes to be successful in it.

HEY BOSS, DID YOU SEE THIS STORY ABOUT—OOPS, UH, NOTHING, BOSS

When you're dull, winning the lottery is a yawn. Fine food and beautiful music move you not a bit.

You miss out on a lot when you're born dull, but your lackluster streak may make you a born leader, at least in the business world. A research team at Rush Medical College here has found that dull people are likely to pass fun-loving, Goodtime Charlies on the corporate ladder.

The team asked 88 executives at major U.S. companies to rate 36 activities that are usually relished by folks who live with gusto, activities like love-making, winning the lottery, and fine dining.

9

No Distracting Them

The researchers found that those with a "low pleasure capacity" (read: dull) were often the most successful executives. They may be dull, but they can concentrate on their tasks because they won't be distracted by, say, incredible sunsets out their office windows.

David C. Clark, a researcher, recalls one executive who scored pretty high on the dull category. "He couldn't slip into small talk. You would lose him with a joke." In other words, just perfect for the boardroom. "He was well tailored, with a firm handshake, direct eye contact and a crisp, businesslike manner," says Mr. Clark.

At the other extreme were the type of executives who once organized panty raids. For all their bonhomie they tended to have lower salaries, fewer responsibilities, and more complaints about work. These executives with "high pleasure capacity" are too busy having fun to do any real work.

A Theory of Dullness

Further (here comes the dull part of the story), fun-seeking executives may be overcompensating for work-related problems. A quest for pleasure may be "an immature struggle to cover up their stress," says Mr. Clark. The dull don't expect much out of life, so they aren't as vulnerable to corporate pitfalls.

Some personnel offices are experimenting with the test, but not all executives are comfortable with its conclusions. "I don't think there's a common thread or logical conclusion that one can reach by looking at someone's personal demeanor to determine whether he's a good manager," says H. Patrick Parrish, executive director of the Chief Executives Forum, an organization of corporate leaders. A good executive, he says, "can work hard and play hard."

Mr. Parrish hasn't yet taken the test.

—Sheila Johnson, in Wall Street Journal, *July 11, 1985, 2:25. Reprinted by permission of* Wall Street Journal, *copyright © Dow Jones & Company, Inc. 1985. All rights reserved.*

KEY ESSAY   *≠ Good*

Think of a workplace you know well—a place you have a job now or had one in the past. If your primary work is being a student, then school is your workplace. Your essay will have two parts:

1. **Introduction:** Identify and briefly explain your role at the workplace ("I am a cashier, salesperson, and general troubleshooter at Pet Supply"). Then name two or three personal qualities that make for success in that job ("To work at Pet Supply, you need to be loyal and good at math and like people as much as you like animals").

2. **Body:** For each quality you named, give one example of how it is important in the job. Think of a specific time when each quality was needed. Tell the story of how you or your co-workers showed the quality (or, unfortunately, showed a lack of it). Here's a sample of such a paragraph showing how a Pet Supply worker must like people as well as animals:

> On Saturdays, with the kids out of school, the dog owners lined up to have their Fifis and Heidis groomed, and the nine-to-five crowd free to run errands, the pet store can get really out of hand. The store fills to the walls with people who have a thousand questions, and all of them want answers right now. The puppies whine until some softhearted child lets all ten out at once, and little Pekinese and cocker spaniels weave in between panty-hosed ankles, leaving surprises everywhere. Birds screech, children yell and giggle, and mothers reprimand. Intermittent squeals come from the snake room. Meanwhile, I need to deal with the hysterical customers—a little girl whose goldfish died in the cold snap last week, a teenager who needs ear-mite medication explained, a woman who needs one of the four schnauzers named Heidi groomed, and a man whose Rottweiler snapped our strongest and most expensive tie-out chain. Somehow, I get all of these people taken care of, get the puppies fed and cleaned up, straighten the store after the rush is over, and still like to be around people and animals when the day is over—after a few hours to myself, that is.

If your example is as long as the preceding one, give it its own paragraph. If your examples are only two sentences each, try to expand them by thinking of more details that will give your classmates the sights, sounds, and feel of your work.

QUESTIONS FOR ANALYZING WRITING

After your class has finished writing, exchange essays with someone else. Read your partner's essay, and then write sentences answering the following questions:

ditto for Friday

1. What are the three qualities needed for the job? What other qualities seem necessary as well?
2. Which example do you like best? Why?
3. Which example could be expanded? Write some questions about details that will help your partner expand the example. For instance, "How many people do you think were in the pet shop altogether? How do you keep calm? What did the crowd look like?"

Return your partner's paper and get your own back. Using the questions your partner wrote, expand one of your examples.

EXERCISES

SET A: WRITING FLUENTLY

1. Interview two people about their jobs. Using the following scales, ask them to identify where on the dotted line they would place the ideal person for their job. Ask them to talk about why they make each choice. Take notes. Choose one interview as subject matter. From your notes and the scales, write a profile of "The Perfect Person to Work at _____."

Cooperative . . . . Competitive
Forceful . . . . Compliant
Assertive . . . . Docile
Dreamy . . . . Realistic
Individualistic . . . . Conformist
Restless . . . . Calm
Humorous . . . . Serious

Flashy .... Bland
Physical .... Intellectual
Warm .... Cool
Sensitive .... Hard-shelled

2. Write one page about frustrations at work. What frustrations *Free*
do you have in your job? How do you deal with them? Do you think
you handle them well or poorly? If poorly, what could you do to
improve?

3. Describe in detail one operation you do at work. If you're a
student, for example, you might tell how you study for a test. Here's
a description of several steps that happen at a boiled-egg factory
(this sample doesn't use the word *I*, but you can if you want to).

BOILED-EGG PEELERS AIM FOR PERFECTION, AND THAT'S NO YOLK

Every day, the company boils batches of 270 dozen eggs
for 25 to 30 minutes per batch. "They peel better if you boil
them that long," says Derrick Ivey, plant manager and son of
the president. Once the eggs are cooked, a pulley lifts and
moves them down the line to be dunked in a big tank of cool
water. Then they are ready for peeling.

The peelers, working six on a shift, get about 15 dozen eggs
apiece. Each batch gets peeled in 15-minute segments. After
a short break, the workers start again.

New employees are required to peel 20 eggs a minute. "A
real clumsy person couldn't do this," says one peeler. Most
workers who stay on at Atlantic strive to be the best. The
current target is Miss Avant's 48-eggs-a-minute record.

Peelers do more than just peel. They inspect the eggs for
sticky little pieces of shell and check for tears in the egg white.
Then they sort the eggs rapidly.

Perfect eggs go in the pail set aside for egg-pickling
companies. (Pickled eggs are a specialty in some taverns,
and Atlantic can charge more for eggs destined for pickling.)
Eggs with slight tears go to salad-bar suppliers. Smashed or
otherwise messy eggs go in the pail for makers of egg salad
and potato salad.

SET B: WRITING ACCURATELY

1. The following words appear in the essay about business executives at the beginning of this chapter:

lackluster   gusto
relished   bonhomie
demeanor   incredible
vulnerable   distracted

Using your dictionary, find a synonym (another word meaning almost the same thing) for each. Here's a sample dictionary entry (Figure 2–1) from the *American Heritage Dictionary* with significant parts labeled.

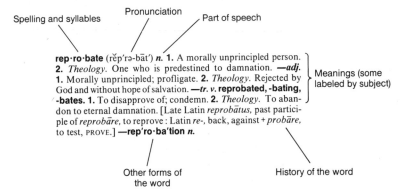

Figure 2–1   Copyright © 1979 by Houghton Mifflin Company. Reprinted by permission from the *American Heritage Dictionary of the English Language, New College Edition.*

After choosing the synonyms, write sentences of your own using each of the words in the list and each of your chosen synonyms in a reasonable way. Notice as you work through this exercise that synonyms are not always interchangeable.

EXAMPLE: lackluster   synonym—dull

1. Clyde might have found a better job except for his *lackluster* grades.
2. That TV miniseries about the Civil War was deadly *dull*.

2. Study the two *Wall Street Journal* articles in this chapter, and notice how direct quotations are punctuated. As you fill in the blanks in the following paragraph, you may need to look back at these articles to be sure your answers are correct.

A quoted statement that stops at the end of a sentence is followed by a _____ and then by the _____ _____ mark. But a quoted statement that ends by telling who said it is followed by a _____ and then the _____ _____ mark. If just a few words are quoted in the middle of a sentence, only the _____ marks are used. A quotation that begins after a statement of who said it will have a _____ before the _____ mark.

3. Write down as accurately as possible an overheard conversation, using quotation marks to enclose the spoken words. If you have access to a tape recorder, you may want to record a brief conversation and then transcribe it. Include at total of at least six quotations from two, possibly three, speakers, and make sure you get the punctuation right. If you want to explain a bit how this conversation took place, write a sentence or two providing background before you begin the dialog. Here's an example to let you see exactly how the punctuation should go.

[A surgeon, making his hospital rounds, is replacing the dressings of a blind patient whose legs have been amputated.]

"Anything more I can do for you?" I ask.
For a long moment he is silent.
"Yes," he says at last and without the least irony. "You can bring me a pair of shoes."
In the corridor, the head nurse is waiting for me.
"We have to do something about him," she says. "Every morning he orders scrambled eggs for breakfast, and, instead of eating them, he picks up his plate and throws it against the wall."
"Throws his plate?"
"Nasty. That's what he is. No wonder his family doesn't come to visit. They probably can't stand him any more than we can."
She is waiting for me to do something.
"Well?"
"We'll see," I say.

—Richard Selzer, "The Discus Thrower." Reprinted by permission of Georges Borchardt, Inc. and the author. Copyright © 1977 by Richard Selzer. Originally appeared in Harper's.

SET C: WRITING LOGICALLY AND COHERENTLY

1. Write separate one-paragraph descriptions of two people who lead their lives in very different ways. For instance, you may know someone who is extremely organized and neat about everything he does, and you may know someone who is very casual and disorderly about the way she conducts her life. Or you could write about a quiet, shy person and an aggressive, outgoing type. When you describe these people, tell how they deal with various areas of their lives: school, work, leisure activities, friendships, finances, dating, religion. Try to draw examples from at least five different areas to illustrate the extreme differences in the way these two people handle the details of their lives.

2. Compose a conversation between the two people you have just described. Create a specific conflict for them to talk about. Here are some suggestions: how much to tip an inattentive waiter; how often to clean the bathroom in the apartment they share; whether or not to work overtime without pay on a job that has to be completed for their company; whether or not to attend a party on the night before a big test.

When you write your conversation, you need to punctuate it accurately. Look at the example in exercise 3 of Set B in this chapter. Notice also that in order to help your readers follow the conversation, you start a new paragraph whenever the speaker changes. Here's another example of a correctly presented conversation—this one between a teacher and a student who has just turned in a paper:

> "Here's my paper. I'm sorry I didn't make it to class. I overslept."
>
> The teacher takes the paper and frowns. "Bob, this is written in pencil."
>
> Bob shrugs. "Sorry. I couldn't find my pen this morning." He waits, then adds, "I can do it over for you."
>
> The teacher shakes his head. "Bob, this is the middle of the semester. You know not to write in pencil."
>
> "Well, I couldn't find my pen. Why do we have to write in pen anyway?"
>
> "I've told you," the teacher answered. "Pencil is too light; I have a lot of papers to read. When can you recopy this?" He hands the paper to the student.
>
> "I don't know—in a couple of days, I guess."

"Bob! This paper was due this morning."
"Yeah, but it'll take me a while to find my pen."
The teacher laughs and takes the paper back. "Go find your pen, Bob. I'll hang on to this for you."

3. Reread the opening two paragraphs in the essay about business executives at the beginning of this chapter. Then, rewrite in your own words the sentence that begins "A research team at Rush Medical College ...".

We've divided the essay's opening into five main parts. Now look at the following summary of the first five parts and notice how the author gets from a general subject to a specific point:

GENERAL SUBJECT	SPECIFIC POINT
1. When *you're dull* ⟶	winning is a yawn.
2. Fine food, beautiful music ⟶	don't move *you*.
3. *You* miss a lot ⟶	when *you're dull*.
BUT	
4. *Your dullness* ⟶	may make *you* a leader in *business*.
5. Researchers found ⟶	*dull* people may do better in *corporations*.

Write your answers to these questions:

- Why is the word *dull* repeated three times?
- Why are the words *you* and *your* used so often in the first four parts?
- What does *but* mean? Why is it placed where it is?
- How would you describe the strategy or design of the first three parts?
- How is the fifth part different from the first four? What words in the previous parts does it not repeat? What new words are introduced?
- Can you explain why the fifth part is different? Try.

When you have finished analyzing the opening, turn to the essay's closing two paragraphs. What has the author done to bring her essay to an interesting and definite close? The article is about a rating scale for measuring dullness and relating it to corporate success, yet the author closes with quotations from an executive who doesn't agree with the results of the survey. Why did she include his comments? What is the impact of the very last sentence? Why is it placed in a paragraph all by itself?

CHAPTER SUMMARY

In this chapter you've studied

- using examples in an explanation
- evaluating another writer's examples
- choosing precise words
- punctuating quotations
- writing dialog
- constructing effective openings and closings

3

PUPPIES AND SLIME: DESCRIPTION WITH FEELING

Relax: you don't have to write an essay about puppies and slime. Those are two words, though, that demonstrate one of the principles you'll use in your essay for this chapter. The principle is that words almost always have feelings associated with them as well as plain old definitions. Let's admit it, the word *puppies* makes all but the hardest of hearts feel like smiling. And the word *slime* makes us feel creepy, whether we're thinking of the actual goop or the kind of person it describes. If you like okra, you will describe the liquid inside it as *juice*; if you detest okra, you might call the same stuff *slime*.

When you wrote your essay about work for the last chapter, no doubt you made use of the feelings that words bring forth. Our example in Chapter 2 about the pet supply store uses words that get across a hectic mood. Look back to that example and see if you can identify a few.

The key essay you will write now encourages you to use words that get across feelings as well as visual images.

KEY ESSAY

Look at the two photographs we've published here. First, give each one a title that you feel expresses the mood or atmosphere of the picture. The title will probably be a general word or phrase that describes an emotion or state of mind. Write your titles on a piece of scratch paper, and put it aside for now.

Now, choose one of the pictures to write about—maybe the one you found easiest to title is the right choice, but maybe the harder one will give you more to write about. Your essay should give a detailed description of this picture to someone who has never seen it. The description should be so careful that it would differentiate this picture from other ones like it—that is, if your readers were to look at five country scenes, they could pick out this particular one.

In your description get across the feeling or state of mind you used in your title. Be sure to use words that are very specific and have strong associations (brutish, queasy, murky, angel, burden, curse, for example, have strong associations). Try to make your description at least a page long by going over your first draft and

adding details, as you learned to do in Chapters 1 and 2. Don't write your title at the top of the essay.

QUESTIONS FOR ANALYZING WRITING

First, exchange papers with a student who did not choose the same picture you did. Read the paper and answer these questions on a separate sheet.

1. What title do you think your partner gave the picture?
2. Copy four of your partner's words or phrases that made you answer question 1 the way you did.
3. Did the writer feel the same way about the picture as you did? What is your title for the picture?

Return the essay and your responses to your partner. Find a new partner who wrote about the same picture you did and exchange essays with him or her. Write answers to these questions.

1. What title do you think your partner gave the photo? Is it close to the title you gave?
2. Copy four of your new partner's words or phrases that help create the mood.
3. Name a basic similarity between your essay and your partner's. Name a difference.
4. Did your partner use a certain order in the description—right to left, foreground to background, general to specific, sky to ground? Did you?

Trade back papers and responses and discuss them with your partner, focusing on whether each of you got across the feeling you wanted to capture. Rewrite your paper before you hand it in.

EXERCISES

SET A: WRITING FLUENTLY

1. Most poetry depends heavily on using words that call forth feelings instead of telling about them. In the poem "A Blessing,"

James Wright describes a beautiful experience that gives him deep happiness. The last lines of the poem are

> Suddenly I realize
> That if I stepped out of my body I would break
> Into blossom.

> —*Copyright* © *1961 by James Wright. Reprinted from* A Branch Will Not Break *by permission of Wesleyan University Press. "A Blessing" first appeared in* Poetry.

What a way to say "I feel great!"

The image of "breaking into blossom" appeals to the senses of touch, sight, and even smell, as well as bringing out our positive associations with flowers—spring, love, happiness, natural beauty.

In this exercise you will play with sensory associations by writing *five-sense poems*. These are fun, fill-in-the-blank poems that are sometimes clinkers but surprisingly often hit on apt images. Here is the form:

_____ looks _____. [The first word has to be an emotion, state of mind, mood, or atmosphere. The second blank must be filled with a color.]
It sounds _____. [Put any number of words in the blank—make it as specific as possible.]
It smells _____.
It tastes _____.
It feels _____.

Here is an example:

> Boredom is gray.
> It sounds like the wind across Nebraska.
> It smells stale.
> It tastes like cold toast with no butter.
> It feels hard and dry.

Well, it's hardly a James Wright poem, but it does get the images flowing. Now you try. Write four five-sense poems. Then exchange poems with a partner. Mark the writer's best poem, and write a sentence explaining your choice.

2. In this exercise you will identify and explain some of the effective word choices in poetry. First, read both of the following

excerpts. The first one is from "Auto Wreck" by Karl Shapiro.

> Its quick soft silver bell beating, beating,
> And down the dark one ruby flare
> Pulsing out red light like an artery,
> The ambulance at top speed floating down
> Past beacons and illuminated clocks
> Wings in a heavy curve, dips down,
> And brakes speed, entering the crowd.
> The doors leap open, emptying light;
> Stretchers are laid out, the mangled lifted
> And stowed into the little hospital.
> Then the bell, breaking the hush, tolls once,
> And the ambulance with its terrible cargo
> Rocking, slightly rocking, moves away,
> As the doors, an afterthought, are closed.

—From "Auto Wreck" in Collected Poems 1940–1978 *by Karl Shapiro.*
Copyright 1978 by Random House, Inc.

The second excerpt is from "Piano" by D. H. Lawrence:

Softly, in the dusk, a woman is singing to me;
Taking me back down the vista of years, till I see
A child sitting under the piano, in the boom of the tingling strings
And pressing the small, poised feet of a mother who smiles as she
  sings.

In spite of myself, the insidious mastery of song
Betrays me back, till the heart of me weeps to belong
To the old Sunday evenings at home, with winter outside
And hymns in the cozy parlour, the tinkling piano our guide.

—From The Complete Poems of D. H. Lawrence, *Collected and Edited by*
Vivian de Sola Pinto and F. Warren Roberts. Copyright © 1964, 1971 by
Angelo Ravagli and C. M. Weekley, Executors of The Estate of Frieda
Lawrence Ravagli. Reprinted by permission of Viking Penguin Inc.

Both of these passages contain words and phrases that appeal to our senses and have emotional connotations. Choose one of the passages; read it again, marking words and phrases that you find especially effective; then write a paragraph in which you do these three things:

a. Name the mood or atmosphere you get from the passage.

b. Choose four or five words or phrases that appeal to your senses and your emotional associations.

c. Explain the sensory and emotional appeal of these terms, relating them to the overall atmosphere you first named.

3. Write a long paragraph capturing the mood of a specific place at a specific time—for example, a dentist's waiting room with several people waiting, a classroom before a big exam, a locker room before a challenging game (or after a loss), a supermarket at 5 P.M. on Friday (or some other hour and day). Try to get across the mood without actually naming it: use specific details, comparisons, and emotionally associated words instead. Trade paragraphs with a partner and see whether you can guess the mood in her or his paper.

SET B: WRITING ACCURATELY

1. Because verbs show the action in a sentence, they give it life. They tell what the sentence says about a subject, so they're also most important in meaning.

Here are two tests for identifying verbs:

a. Verbs can be put in past, present, and future (Herman *was*, Herman *is*, Herman *will be*; the chauffeur *drove*, the chauffeur *drives*, the chauffeur *will drive*). *Herman* and *chauffeur* are the subjects.

b. Verbs sound right with nouns (ladies, fellow, blossom, Arthur) or pronouns (he, they, that, she, it) ahead of them.

Using both of these tests, which words in the following list could be verbs?

had	awful
is	climb
elephant	step
interest	far
slip	kindly

Some words, you realize, can be used as either verbs or nouns (interest, slip, climb, and step, for example). You need to look at the whole sentence to decide. Try to identify the verbs in the following passage:

The cloud floated there to one side like the bolster on his grandmother's bed. It went over a cabin on the edge of a hill, where two bare chinaberry trees clutched at the sky. He drove through a heap of dead oak leaves, his wheels stirring their weightless sides to make a silvery melancholy whistle as the car passed through their bed. No car had been along this way ahead of him. Then he saw that he was on the edge of a ravine that fell away, a red erosion, and that this was indeed the road's end.

He pulled the brake. But it did not hold, though he put all his strength into it. The car tipped toward the edge, rolled a little. Without doubt, it was going over the bank.

—From "Death of a Traveling Salesman" in A Curtain of Green, *copyright 1941, 1969 by Eudora Welty. Reprinted by permission of Harcourt Brace Jovanovich, Inc.*

With three or four other students, discuss your choice. There are sixteen verbs; three of them are two-word verbs. Infinitives, like *to move, to go, to drink, to procrastinate,* don't count as verbs in sentences.

2. In other languages, as you probably know, sometimes adjectives have to change their endings according to the nouns they go with:

- los muchachos perditos (the lost children, in Spanish)
- las muchachas perditas (the lost girls)
- les enfants perdus (the lost children, in French)
- l'enfant perdu (the lost child)

Luckily, in English we only have to match up subjects and verbs according to *singular* (child, lily) and *plural* (children, lilies). See whether you can choose which verbs aren't right in the following sentences. (The subjects are underlined once and the verbs twice.)

a. Sue likes computer programming less than she likes sketching.
b. Her sketches are unrecognizable blotches.
c. The flowers that she drew for Betty was difficult to identify.
d. Literature and exotic dance is her favorite subjects.
e. No wonder people loves to talk with Sue.
f. Betty and Bobby enjoy Sue's company, as she drinks coffee and delight them with her stories.

In a small group or individually, write explanations for why the verbs you chose don't sound right.

Make up sentences using the following phrases—exactly—as beginnings. Be sure the verb you choose matches the subject(s).

a. The compact disk player and the video cassette recorder
b. Our cat Clyde
c. Both Clyde and the dog Toke
d. People who
e. The good points of our society

3. Work the following verbs into a short paragraph. You *don't* have to use the exact form we print here; you can change a verb's form or tense to fit your paragraph. Be sure it remains a verb, though, and doesn't slip into a noun or adjective usage.

VERBS TO USE

watch   wonder
feel   forget
amuse

SET C: WRITING LOGICALLY AND COHERENTLY

1. Look carefully at a work of art: a painting or a sculpture. (Four paintings are reproduced here.) Take notes or free write about what the work looks like, how it makes you feel, and what it makes you think about. Organize and develop this material into a two-paragraph essay, in which the first paragraph clearly describes the work of art and the second paragraph identifies and explains your reactions to it. As you go over your first draft, try to make sure that your reader could understand your essay without ever seeing the artwork.

2. In your next two-paragraph essay you will divide your paragraphs into *objective* description and *subjective* description. Objective writing aims to leave out emotional associations and suggestive phrasing; it is plain, detailed, and direct. Newspaper reporters and business writers frequently try to write objectively. Subjective writing adds the author's feelings about the content by appealing to emotions and senses, often through vivid word choice.

Chagall, Marc. *I and the Village*.
1911. Oil on canvas, 6′3 5/8″ ×
59 5/8″. Collection, The Museum
of Modern Art, New York.
Mrs. Simon Guggenheim Fund.
Photograph © 1987 The Museum
of Modern Art, New York.

Rousseau, Henri. *The Sleeping
Gypsy*. 1897. Oil on canvas,
51″ × 6′7″. Collection, The
Museum of Modern Art, New
York. Gift of Mrs. Simon
Guggenheim.

Henri de Toulouse-Lautrec, *At the Moulin Rouge*, 1892, oil on canvas, 48 1/2 × 55 3/8″, Helen Birch Bartlett Memorial Collection, 1928.610. Copyright © The Art Institute of Chicago. All Rights Reserved. Courtesy of The Art Institute of Chicago.

Bartolome Esteban Murillo, *A Girl and Her Duenna*. Circa 1670. Canvas, 1.277 × 1.061 (50 1/4 × 41 3/4 in.). National Gallery of Art, Washington. Widener Collection.

Here, for example, are two paragraphs that both give instruction to a beginner. You'll find it easy to tell which is the more objective and which is the more subjective.

> At one time or another, you may need to put all of the fixtures, appliances, faucets and pipes in your plumbing system out of operation. When you do major repairs or installations that call for cutting into the main pipes, or when you need to clear and recharge waterlogged air chambers, you must both shut off the incoming water and drain out the existing supply before you can start work. When you leave a house empty and un-heated for the winter, you must also weatherproof the system to protect it from bursting in freezing temperatures.
>
> — *"Shutting Down the Plumbing System,"* Plumbing *(Alexandria, Va.: Time-Life Books), 17.*

> Think of the picture you want to draw as of a melody drawn on white paper. The black ink is the medium by which the melody is seen instead of heard. If the lines are drawn with the same speed, the melody will be monotonous. Each tune and picture is individual. As in music, color and brush-stroke make a per-fect combination and a wonderful rhythm. It is difficult to explain in words the effect of the change of color caused by the speed of the brush. The understanding develops only through repeated practice of simple flowing lines.
>
> — *"The Tempo of Strokes,"* Japanese Ink-Painting *(Rutland, Vt.: Charles E. Tuttle, 1959), 32.*

For this exercise, write one objective paragraph and then one subjective paragraph about the same thing: a food or a meal. The first paragraph must give an exact description of the food or meal and should not convey your feelings about it at all. The second paragraph should also describe the same thing, but your feel-ings—positive, negative, bored, anxious, disappointed, delighted, whatever—should come through.

3. Magazine advertisements strive to impress you deeply within the very few moments that you glance at them. Thus, they use strongly emotional pictures, colors, and words to quickly create a mood or atmosphere that the advertisers want you to associate with their product. Find a magazine ad that has a strong atmosphere, and write a paragraph identifying the atmosphere and explaining what elements of the ad contribute to it.

CHAPTER SUMMARY

In this chapter you've studied

- using words to get across mood
- writing five-sense poems
- identifying, explaining, and using language that appeals to senses and emotions
- identifying verbs and using verbs that match their subjects
- using objective and subjective language in a description

4

WHAT DO YOU KNOW?: INFORMATIVE WRITING

Emotional appeal makes a piece of writing interesting, but so do other elements. If you were in the market for a compact disk player, an utterly emotionless review of a certain brand would still be fascinating to you. As you read the following article, think about what makes it appealing.

AD DIRECTORS FUSS OVER FOODS AS MUCH AS OVER LIVE MODELS

Loretta Swit, Mr. T and other celebrities ham it up on some new Burger King commercials. But the real star of the ads is the Whopper, which was recently beefed up to provide stiffer competition for Wendy's and the Big Mac.

Using a special lens, director Elbert Budin filmed the burger from less than an inch away to make it look gargantuan. To create an ideal bun, extra sesame seeds were pasted on with tweezers and egg white. Water was squirted on the tomatoes to give them a "dewy, fresh look," and the condiments were dabbed on meticulously with Q-tips. Says Mr. Budin: "We tried to get the Whopper as perfect as possible without making it appear pristine. Food must always remain earthy and approachable."

Although shooting pictures of food and beverages may seem rudimentary, advertisers fuss as much over corn flakes and TV dinners as they do over stunning fashion models. The lighting in a recent Wendy's commercial was done by John Alcott, winner of an Academy Award for his cinematography for the movie *Barry Lyndon*. On the Duncan Hines account at Saatchi & Saatchi Compton Inc., employees are required to bake brownies and blueberry muffins themselves to get to know the products intimately. Even Vice Chairman Phillip Voss spent an afternoon flipping hamburgers for Krystal's, the agency's fast-food restaurant client.

"It's much more interesting to work all day with Christie Brinkley than with a tomato," says Charles Piccirillo, executive creative director at Leber Katz partners, an ad agency. "But food can really look bland on a big TV screen if you don't pay attention to the tiniest of details."

The aim of food advertising, of course, is to make people lick their chops and rush out to a restaurant or supermarket. Seldom are actors in commercials shown eating food because that might turn consumers off. "People shoving food in their mouths isn't the greatest thing to look at," Mr. Voss says. "What you want to do is move the camera in close and make love to the product." But increasingly the food in commercials does more than just sit there and look succulent. Recently, there have been flying potato chips and pickles, talking sandwiches and a bacon cheeseburger cruising along an expressway.

"That stuff is as expensive as blazes," says Paul Mulcahy, president of Campbell Soup Co.'s in-house advertising agency. "You have to wonder if a nicely decorated plate isn't as effective as food hurtling through the air."

But even simple advertisements can be painstaking ordeals because food products seldom behave the way directors want. For one thing, food is very temperamental under hot lights. Directors say they must be careful that the tops of hamburger buns don't dry out and cave in or that raw meat doesn't turn a sickly brown. They also must be sure that beer gushes into a mug at just the right speed and with just the right amount of head.

No one knows more about such challenges than Ralcie Ceass, supervisor of food photography at General Mills Inc. For a typical Bisquick TV commercial, she may cook 1,000 pancakes to come up with enough that have a smooth contour and golden-brown color. "It's especially important that food looks gorgeous on package labels," she says, "because the box sits on the grocery shelf for days surrounded by competing brands."

Indeed, Victor Scocozza, who does package shots, says some finicky ad agency people insist that he photograph a piece of cake on a plate first with four crumbs, then eight crumbs, then 12 crumbs. He once spent 7 1/2 hours on a single chocolate-chip cookie.

In trying to glorify food, companies may go too far. Last year the Council of Better Business Bureaus concluded that ads for Old El Paso sauce misrepresented the thickness of the product. The council also objected to a Mauna Loa commercial that seemed to show only whole macadamia nuts. A consumer had complained that jars typically contain many broken nuts.

"But by and large, advertisements are far more honest today than they were 10 years ago," says Marianne Langan, a so-called food stylist who gussies up food for photo sessions. "Years ago, we would have used milk of magnesia in a picture for cream of mushroom soup."

Campbell Soup was cited in 1969 by the Federal Trade Commission for adding marbles to bowls of vegetable soup so it would look chunkier. Now, the company says, it polices its advertising scrupulously. To ensure that the soup shown in ads is representative, the company purchases it at random in grocery stores. Vegetables and meat are evenly split between the two bowls that come from each can. And top marketing and legal executives scrutinize proofs of each ad to make sure that during the printing process a pale yellow broth doesn't magically turn golden.

While fewer ads are downright misleading these days, companies still fudge a lot. For example, maraschino-cherry syrup is painted on ham for appetite appeal. Some products are sprayed with glycerin to make them glisten. Cigarette smoke and humidifiers are used to simulate steam for baked goods. And plastic sometimes substitutes for ice. Director Lee Howard even vacuums individual corn flakes and applies a chemical fixative so that when they are poured from a box and collide in mid-air, little pieces don't break off. "We never actually cheat," Mr. Howard says. "We merely handle the food in a different way than a housewife would."

Why did the *Wall Street Journal's* editors think that this article would have wide appeal? Well, they probably considered that this is a subject that not many people know the details about, but it certainly touches almost everyone's life. The wealth of examples (which many readers would recognize) and quotations from experts keep the article entertaining. What do you find the most interesting example used? Compare your response with your classmates'. Why do you think people react differently?

KEY ESSAY

Write an informative essay about a subject that others in your class may not know as well as you do. "But I don't have any special knowledge!" you may complain. This is a case for some brain-storming, because of course you have a specialty. Here are some categories of special knowledge and some possibilities under each.

WORK

- Problems of water treatment
- Techniques in selling furniture
- Toilet training a child
- Library card catalogs
- Getting a meal on the table all hot at the same time
- Scheduling studying, housework, or other tasks
- Laying out a newspaper page

HOBBIES, SKILLS, RECREATION

- Kinds of watercolor paper
- How to plan a great weekend in Chicago (or another city)
- Pottery

- Photography
- Throwing a party
- Wallpapering a room
- Detective fiction

STUDIES AND SPECIAL INTERESTS

- Genetic engineering
- Word processing
- Persuasive speaking
- 1940s fashions
- Hospital care
- Tuna farming
- Dialects of English
- How movie previews are made
- Epilepsy

For On Wed – in class

Make your own lists using these three categories. Then choose two or three topics and for each, complete a five-minute free writing. (See Chapter 1, Set A, exercise 2, for an explanation of free writing.) If the topic you can develop most effectively for your essay isn't clear to you from rereading your free writings, ask a friend or classmate to read them and choose for you.

As you make notes for your essay, make use of some of the approaches Alsop uses:

- Explaining processes — *how to do it*
- Explaining principles — *how it works*
- Identifying problems
- Relating history — *how it was done in past*
- Describing new trends — *in work/field/hobby*

Group your notes into related batches, and from those write at least two pages on the topic you selected.

QUESTIONS FOR ANALYZING WRITING

Read a classmate's essay, and write the answers to these questions.

1. Did you learn something from this essay that you didn't already know? What? Do you want to learn more?

2. Would you call this writing mostly subjective or mostly objective? (If you didn't do Set C, exercise 2 in Chapter 3, read the explanation of *subjective* and *objective* there.) Why? Whichever it is, is it appropriate to the writer's subject?
3. Are there questions you'd like to ask about the writer's subject— more examples, details, explanations, and so on? If so, list your questions.

When you get your paper and your partner's responses back, try to make the desired additions to your essay before you submit it to your instructor.

EXERCISES

SET A: WRITING FLUENTLY

1. Write a short paragraph about a recurring problem in your life. Here's an example:

> A small but recurring problem in my life is the white tile on my kitchen floor. My child is too preoccupied with other things to notice that he often messes it up, and to make matters worse, the back door opens right into the kitchen, so everyone brings in dirt. It's impossible to keep perfectly clean, and I've stopped trying.

Now, expand that short paragraph by substituting specific details and examples for general statements, like this:

> A small but recurring problem in my life is the pure white tile floor in my apartment kitchen. When my seventeen-year-old son stands by the counter eating a chili dog, I try to pay attention to his enthusiastic talk about his computer program instead of to the goop dripping out of the bun onto the white floor. To make matters worse, the back door opens directly into the kitchen, and at least seven times a day during the winter people track in mud, salt, slush, cinders, and snow. The doormat retires into a sodden wet heap after the first two assaults, no matter what I do. Maybe Superwoman or Supernag could keep this white floor clean, but I'm not interested in being either one.

2. Write a letter to someone much like yourself who hasn't yet taken college courses. In the letter inform your reader about some aspect of college life or classes that he or she may not be aware of.

3. During one whole day, keep a record of all the new information you come across. Write down where the information came from (newspaper, book, magazine, TV news, TV program, teacher, friends' conversation, eavesdropping, and so on). What information was most objectively presented? What was least objectively presented? Mark these on your record. Write two or three sentences telling what you learned from making this list.

Friday

SET B: WRITING ACCURATELY　(*Do*)　*Apostrophes*

1. In the following phrases why do words end in 's?

- the sales clerk's pitch, one year's time, for heaven's sake, Susie's Cafe, Tom's friend's apartment, a stone's throw

    Try to write phrases meaning the same thing without using 's. You will probably need to rearrange and add words like *of* or *belonging to*.
    In the next group of items, why are apostrophes used?

- can't tell a lie, what he'd done, you'll be surprised, haven't a penny, it's not true, she's right

    Try to rewrite these without using apostrophes. You won't need to rearrange, but you'll end up with more words.
    Why do the following words groups have no apostrophes in them?

- among good friends, horses for sale, ups and downs, he calls us girls, makes the grade, fixes the phone line

The first two groups you looked at included singular *possessives* and *contractions*: look those words up in your dictionary and see whether you can sharpen your original answers. The third word group (among good friends, etc.) includes neither possessives nor contractions: the *s* endings you see there indicate plural nouns (showing more than one) or third person singular verb forms (I cry, you cry, he *cries*, I eat well, you eat well, she *eats* well). These uses of the letter *s* in English don't require an apostrophe. One might wish that *-s* weren't such a busy ending in the language; unfortunately, we don't get to change these things to suit ourselves.

2. Find the contractions in Alsop's *Wall Street Journal* article. Copy them, and next to each one write out the phrase it stands for.

3. Write a list of six word groups that use plural words ending in *s* (example: ladies of the house). Then write a list of six word groups that use possessives ending in *'s* (example: a poet's delicacy).

4. Write a paragraph on the subject of "How I Wake Up," using at least two possessives ending in *'s* and at least four contractions. Then write the same paragraph without using possessives and contractions. When you read your two paragraphs aloud, what is the difference in the way they sound?

SET C: WRITING LOGICALLY AND COHERENTLY

1. Your goal is to explain to a classmate an old way you had and a new way you have of doing something. Write a paragraph about each way. Did you describe your old way first and then your new one, or vice versa? Try reading your two paragraphs in both orders: old-new and new-old. What changes would you need to make to reverse your original order? Which order do you think is more effective? Why?

2. Brainstorm a list of things that frustrate you or make you angry. If you'd like, ask a friend to help you make the list. Then rewrite the list in order from the least bothersome thing to the most bothersome. Using that list, write a paragraph.

3. Here is a group of sentences that will go together into a coherent paragraph, but we've scrambled them. See whether you can number them so that the sequence makes sense.

● _____ This time, I reset it for eight, rationalizing away the list of things I was going to do in the extra hour or so.
● _____ If I have to get up at 8:00 A.M., I set the alarm for 6:30 A.M.,

thinking I can spend the time writing, cleaning, or otherwise being productive.
- _____ Once I'm back beneath my covers, I doze on and off for the painfully short thirty minutes, leaping out to the alarm as soon as it resumes its lament.
- _____ I have to keep my alarm clock as far away from my bed as possible; otherwise I turn it off without waking up.
- _____ At eight, I have to get up, or I'll be late, so I finally trudge grimly to the bathroom.
- _____ Getting out of bed in the morning is an agonizing process for me.
- _____ I think I'm going to have to change my ways, though—I don't think my new roommates will like listening to my alarm three or four times every morning.
- _____ When six thirty arrives, and the alarm begins to shriek at me, I stumble out of bed and set the alarm for seven.

CHAPTER SUMMARY

In this chapter you've studied

- identifying a topic of special interest to you
- helping another writer explain a subject
- expanding a paragraph by using details and examples
- using apostrophes
- deciding the best order for details and examples

5

OF CLUNKERS AND GURKS: DEFINING TERMS

To write clearly you must make sure that your readers will understand the words you use—and understand them with the same meaning that you intend. If you write to your grandmother that you have this *heavy* new heartthrob who is simply a *hunk*, she'll probably envision a man closely resembling a chest of drawers (when all you meant was that you're crazy about this guy who has a great body). Your best friend, of course, would know what you meant. But, since slang is often the language of an in-group, you should be careful about using it in writing. Consider always whether your readers will understand exactly what you mean.

If you want to use words that your readers may not fully understand, take a moment to define those terms. Often you need only a sentence. Notice how neatly *Newsweek*'s movie reviewer slips in his definition of the slang term *clunker*:

> If, as the movie-biz word has it, *Spies Like Us* turns out to be a box-office smash, it won't be the first time that has happened to a clunker. A clunker is a movie that gears up to make you laugh, presses the boffola button and then leaves you hanging, your mouth open and a poor little strangled gurk emerging instead of a full-fledged har-de-har-har.
>
> —*Jack Kroll, "Comedius Interruptus,"* Newsweek, *16 December 1985,* *82.*

Clunker can mean a broken-down car or just something that falls flat, but Kroll neatly defines the term in a different and specific way, telling us exactly what he means. He does not, however, clutter up his paragraph by defining *movie-biz*, *boffola*, *gurk*, or *har-de-har-har* because they are not important to the main point of his review, as *clunker* is. Defining any of those other words would not add to the central meaning of the passage.

Sometimes writers employ definition as the focus of an entire essay. When doing so, they usually are trying to clarify at length some term or concept that is often misunderstood or only partially understood. In the following article, syndicated news columnist William Raspberry wants his readers to rethink the many connotations (i.e., often unconscious emotional associations) that we have in our minds about the term *black*.

VOCABULARY

slander	an insult
quintessentially	most typically
innate	inborn
inculcated	firmly taught
prowess	superior ability
scrimping	economizing severely
elocution	the art of speaking effectively
assumption	idea or judgment accepted as true
concede	grant, give up
perverted	misdirected

Vocab list

Look up in your dictionary any other words in the essay that you do not understand.

THE HANDICAP OF DEFINITION

I know all about bad schools, mean politicians, economic deprivation and racism. Still, it occurs to me that one of the heaviest burdens black Americans—and black children in particular—have to bear is the handicap of definition: the question of what it means to be black.

Let me explain quickly what I mean. If a basketball fan says that the Boston Celtics' Larry Bird plays "black," the fan intends it—and Bird probably accepts it—as a compliment. Tell pop singer Tom Jones he moves "black" and he might grin in appreciation. Say to Teena Marie or The Average White Band that they sound "black" and they'll thank you.

But name one pursuit, aside from athletics, entertainment or sexual performance in which a white practitioner will feel complimented to be told he does it "black." Tell a white broadcaster he talks "black," and he'll sign up for diction lessons. Tell a white reporter he writes "black" and he'll take a writing course. Tell a white lawyer he reasons "black" and he might sue you for slander.

What we have here is a tragically limited definition of blackness, and it isn't only white people who buy it.

Think of all the ways black children can put one another down with charges of "whiteness." For many of these children, hard study and hard work are "white." Trying to please a teacher might be criticized as acting "white." Speaking correct English is "white." Scrimping today in the interest of tomorrow's goals is "white." Educational toys and games are "white."

An incredible array of habits and attitudes that are conducive to success in business, in academia, in the non-entertainment professions are likely to be thought of as somehow "white." Even economic success, unless it involves such "black" undertakings as numbers banking, is defined as "white."

And the results are devastating. I wouldn't deny that blacks often are better entertainers and athletes. My point is the harm that comes from too narrow a definition of what is black.

One reason black youngsters tend to do better at basketball, for instance, is that they assume they can do it well, and so they practice constantly to prove themselves right.

Wouldn't it be wonderful if we could infect black children with the notion that excellence in math is "black" rather than white, or possibly Chinese? Wouldn't it be of enormous value if we could create the myth that morality, strong families, determination, courage and love of learning are traits brought by slaves from Mother Africa and therefore quintessentially black?

There is no doubt in my mind that most black youngsters could develop their mathematical reasoning, their elocution and their attitudes the way they develop their jump shots and their dance steps: by the combination of sustained, enthusiastic practice and the unquestioned belief that they can do it.

In one sense, what I am talking about is the importance of developing positive ethnic traditions. Maybe Jews have an innate talent for communication; maybe Chinese are born with a gift for mathematical reasoning; maybe blacks are naturally blessed with athletic grace. I doubt it. What is at work, I suspect, is assumption, inculcated early in their lives, that this is a thing our people do well.

Unfortunately, many of the things about which blacks make this assumption are things that do not contribute to their career success—except for that handful of the truly gifted who can make it as entertainers and athletes. And many of the things we concede to whites are the things that are essential to economic security.

So it is with a number of assumptions black youngsters make about what it is to be a "man": physical aggressiveness, sexual prowess, the refusal to submit to authority. The prisons are full of people who, by this perverted definition, are unmistakably men.

But the real problem is not so much that the things defined as "black" are negative. The problem is that the definition is much too narrow.

Somehow, we have to make our children understand that they are intelligent, competent people, capable of doing whatever they put their minds to and making it in the American mainstream, not just in the black subculture.

What we seem to be doing, instead, is raising up yet another generation of young blacks who will be failures—by definition.

—*William Raspberry, "Instilling Positive Images,"* The Washington Post, *July 19, 1985, A25. Copyright © 1985, Washington Post Writers Group, reprinted with permission.*

KEY ESSAY

Write an extended definition of some slang term or expression that you use every day (like *nerd, spacey, bubblehead, yuppie, far out, bottom line, smack, slammer, klutz, tacky*).

Or, write an extended definition (similar to William Raspberry's) defining some term that carries strong associations for you, like

machismo, self-esteem, military, femininity, sex appeal, intellectual.
   In composing this paper you'll need to employ some or all of the suggestions that follow.

1. Planning Your Essay

Notes

Before you begin to write, think about what you're going to say, how you're going to say it, and how you're going to end it. Jot down the main ideas you intend to include, and arrange them in a way that seems logical and easy for your readers to follow. Be sure you have enough good, specific examples to make your definition absolutely clear.

2. Starting Your Essay

Before beginning to write, you may want to consult your dictionary or a dictionary of slang or even an encyclopedia to see how your term is defined there. If you find your word, do *not* begin by quoting the dictionary definition—that makes for a fairly boring introduction (unless you are able to continue by telling your readers why that definition won't do). Try, instead, to devise your own one-sentence definition, which you will then proceed to tell more about.

3. Expanding Your Definition

You have several choices of ways to expand your opening definition.

   A. Use Examples. You might continue, as William Raspberry does, by providing a number of specific examples that help to clarify the meaning of the term.

   B. Use Description. You might prefer to continue with descriptive details, as Russell Baker does in this paragraph defining the attributes of the perfect chair for a sidewalk cafe:

> Such a chair must be of wicker construction with the back tilted ever so subtly to encourage surrender from shoulder to hip. The seat must be deep enough to carry the entire load of

the thigh. When sagged into, the chair must produce an inner serenity relieving the mind of niggling worries about time and economics.

—Excerpt from "The Subversive Chair" from No Cause for Panic *by Russell Baker (J. B. Lippincott), p. 31, 1962. Copyright © 1962, 1963, 1964 by The New York Times Company. Reprinted by permission of Harper & Row, Publishers, Inc.*

C. Find Details and Examples. Before you begin writing, think about movies or TV shows you have seen, articles or books you have read, or stories you have heard that might provide examples to include in your paragraph. Think of incidents that have happened in your life that might provide concrete support. Read your chosen topic sentence to a friend or classmate or an instructor in another class, ask him or her to comment on your idea, and write down any interesting answers to use when you write.

D. Use a Single Example. You might choose to flesh out your definition with a single long example, especially if you're defining a term like *klutz*. You simply explain some weird, mindless behavior of your friend Albert that conveys the very essence of klutziness.

E. Point Out Differences. Since a good definition will make clear the difference between the word you are explaining and words with similar meanings, you might want to tell us how being a nerd is different from being spacey.

F. Provide a Contrast. Another way to clarify the difference between things involves explaining what your thing is *not*. For instance, you might point out that being competitive means wanting to win, but it does *not* include cheating or taking an unfair advantage.

4. Concluding Your Essay

Try to conclude your essay by making a point of some sort. It need not be earth shaking. You can simply end by telling why you think that understanding the definition you've just given is important, as Raspberry does, or by telling, in a sentence or two, why you think the word is useful or amusing or damaging or unfair.

QUESTIONS FOR ANALYZING WRITING

Exchange your paper with someone else in the class. Read your partner's definition carefully, and then, on a separate sheet of paper, write responses to the following questions.

1. Does the opening sentence provide a clear basic definition of the term? If not, what isn't clear?
2. What do you like best about this piece of writing?
3. Are there enough specific examples and details to make the meaning clear and the essay interesting? If not, in which paragraphs are more specifics needed? Can you suggest a few good ones?
4. Does the essay have a conclusion—or does it just suddenly end? If you think the closing needs improvement, try to suggest a more effective way to end.

After you receive your partner's comments about your paper, decide which suggestions are valuable and revise accordingly. You may also discover other things that you want to change, add, or rearrange at this time.

EXERCISES

SET A: WRITING FLUENTLY

Monday

1. One of the most important things about writing a good extended definition—or, in fact, about good writing in general—involves coming up with enough specific details to allow your readers to see exactly what you mean. Look back over William Raspberry's essay and count the number of specific examples he includes. How many are there?

The following topic sentences were written by professional writers who supplied abundant examples and specific details to support them. Choose one sentence that interests you, and flesh out a paragraph with your own details.

A cowboy is someone who loves his work.

—*Gretel Ehrlich*

There is something triumphant about a really bad meal.

—Laurie Colwin

Much madness is divinest sense to a discerning eye.

—Emily Dickinson

A role model is an adult person of your own gender whom you admire and want to be like.

—Lois Gould

Goodbyes are never easy—not just the parting but the whole process of leaving a loved one or even a casual acquaintance.

—Laurie Taylor

Money is the new sex in America.

—Liz Smith

2. Write a paragraph defining what it means to be one of the following: an athlete, a cheerleader, a sports fan, a candy striper, a cocktail waitress, a bartender, a sports car owner, a born shopper, a cat lover, a cat hater, a smoker, a collector of something, a trivia expert. You may want to follow some of the suggestions earlier in this chapter under the heading "Finding Details and Examples" before you begin writing.

3. Abstractions—things that exist only in the mind—are some of the most difficult terms to define but also some of the ones that most need defining. Write a paragraph in which you try to define one of these abstract terms: jealousy, boredom, cowardice, egotism, generosity, progress, stupidity, conformity, beauty.

Remember that in order to be effective, your paragraph will need to contain well-chosen specific examples or illustrations, which you will devise by following the advice given earlier in this chapter for "Finding Details and Examples."

SET B: WRITING ACCURATELY

1. Whenever you use pronouns (words like *he, she, it, his, her, their*, etc., that stand in for nouns), you must be sure that each has a clear *antecedent* (the noun that the pronoun stands for). If you

don't, your readers can get lost. Several words, when used as pronouns, are especially treacherous about appearing without specific antecedents: *this*, *which*, and *these*. Whenever you write one of these words as a pronoun, pause and make sure you can name the thing or the idea that *this*, *which*, or *these* refers to.

The following sentences are vague because they contain pronouns without clear antecedents. Rewrite each sentence until it becomes perfectly clear.

Example: Clyde made Gary do his homework.
Revisions: Gary did his homework because Clyde made him.
              Gary did Clyde's homework because Clyde made him.

a. Hampton aced the history test because he made it so easy.
b. Fred is working on the railroad in Tennessee, which depresses him.
c. Imelda dropped out of school after they took away fall break.
d. Norbert chased the ground squirrel until he got tired.
e. Frequently local citizens' groups want to ban Twain's novel *Adventures of Huckleberry Finn*, which many consider his best work. This seems strange.
f. Although Juan's mother is a chemist, Juan hates it.
g. Rosita tried to support herself by painting, then acting, then dancing, and then singing. This was a mistake.
h. Melvin blamed his failure on his choice of occupations, which was unfortunate.
i. Pedro told Barney to start the new tractor because he didn't know how.
j. Washington wore a sombrero and sequined gloves, which were several sizes too large.

2. Read and then rewrite the following paragraph to eliminate all vague pronoun references. You may need to add words, take some out, or rearrange a few.

> Myrtle and Marie were just finishing their second cup of coffee when they told them they would have to leave. They complained that this wasn't fair, which they ignored. This made them furious, so she asked to speak to the manager, which proved a mistake. She came at once and told them sharply that this was an outrage, that the restaurant was closing, and they needed to go home. They argued that this was going to ruin its good reputation because they intended to

tell all their friends about it. She said they could print it in the paper for all she cared, turned on her heel, and left them flabbergasted. Having no other recourse, they paid the bill and stomped out, vowing never to do it again.

3. Write a paragraph that describes an incident involving you and at least two other people. Pay particular attention to your pronouns. Make sure each has a clear antecedent. Use the paragraph you worked on in exercise 2 as your guide.

4. A possessive pronoun should be either singular or plural, depending on whether the word it refers to (its *antecedent*) is singular or plural. Most of the time achieving this *agreement*, as the rule books call it, is easy:

- *People* often care a great deal about *their* pets.
- A *person* often dearly loves *his or her* pet.
- *She* is crazy about *her* cat Moose.
- A *man* is often fond of *his* dog.

But agreement can get complicated when a posssessive pronoun has a pronoun as its antecedent. This is especially true with the pesky "indefinite pronouns," many of which sound plural but are supposed to be singular:

everyone	everybody	someone
anyone	anybody	somebody
no one	one	each
either	neither	

This often illogical rule makes it correct to write,

- *Everyone* should take good care of *his or her* pets.

When talking or when writing to a friend, most of us would say,

- *Everyone* should take good care of *their* pets.

But you may encounter some people who object to the use of *everyone/their* and some who dislike the use of *his or her*. Until fairly recently standard English required the use of the masculine pronoun alone:

- *Everyone* should take good care of *his* pet.

To be on the safe side, avoid the indefinite pronouns when you're writing about people in general. Write in the plural whenever possible:

● *People* should take good care of *their* pets.

Now you'll get to practice your use of pronouns. Write out the following sentences, filling in the blanks with an appropriate pronoun or two. You may prefer to rewrite some of the sentences in the plural.

Example: Every student must show _____ ID to get in.
Revisions: Students must show their IDs to get in.
            Every student must show his or her ID to get in.

a. Everyone must buckle _____ seat belts by law in Texas.
b. Salvador has a new baby, but I haven't seen _____.
c. Liz carried the jar of pickles carelessly, and _____ fell.
d. The conscientious doctor should consider the needs of _____ patients.
e. Our kitty has lost _____ appetite.
f. Someone has locked _____ keys in the car.

5. Look over the papers you have written so far for this class, and find a paragraph in which you used singular pronouns (*I, he, she, it, one,* etc.). Rewrite that paragraph using plural pronouns (*we, they, our, us,* etc.).

SET C: WRITING LOGICALLY AND COHERENTLY

1. Write a paragraph in which you define a term by contrasting it with another quite similar in meaning, like *beautiful* and *handsome, ignorant* and *stupid, sad* and *depressed, lazy* and *irresponsible, assertive* and *aggressive, argue* and *discuss, happy* and *delighted.*

Look up both of the words you choose in a dictionary and then think about the distinctions. Try to come up with several concrete examples to illustrate the meaning of each word. Use the suggestions given earlier in this chapter under the heading "Finding Details and Examples."

After beginning with a general statement like, "Many people fail to understand the difference between being *ignorant* and being *stupid*," you can then arrange your material either of these two ways. You can, if you wish, present your contrast point by point, giving details as you go along: Stupidity is foolish; ignorance is innocent. Stupidity implies lack of intelligence; ignorance implies lack of knowledge. Stupidity is hopeless; ignorance can be fixed. Or, if you find that repeated contrast too challenging, you can first give all your information about stupidity, including examples. Then, with a single transition (like "Ignorance, on the other hand, is not a hopeless condition"), you give all your facts about ignorance, with illustrations in appropriate places.

To produce a nicely unified paragraph, you need only to add at the end a final sentence commenting on how important these differences are or how most people can tolerate ignorance but will not put up with stupidity.

2. The following paragraph, written by Gretel Ehrlich, defines what it means to be a cowboy or rancher by providing a wealth of descriptive details plus a short illustration. Read the paragraph carefully and look up any unfamiliar words in your dictionary when you finish. You should know before you begin, though, that the key word in this definition—*androgynous*—means possessing both male and female characteristics.

> If a rancher or cowboy is thought of as a "man's man"
> —laconic, hard-drinking, inscrutable—there's almost no
> place in which the balancing act between male and female,
> manliness and femininity, can be more natural. If he's gruff,
> handsome, and physically fit, he's androgynous at the core.
> Ranchers are midwives, hunters, nurturers, providers, and
> conservationists, all at once. What we've interpreted as tough-
> ness—weathered skin, calloused hands, a squint in the eye,
> and a growl in the voice—only masks the tenderness inside.
> "Now don't go telling me these lambs are cute," one rancher
> warned me the first day I walked into the football-field-sized
> lambing sheds. The next thing I knew he was holding a black
> lamb. "Ain't this little rat good-lookin'?"

> — *"Revisionist Cowboy," in* The Solace of Open Spaces *by Gretel Ehrlich.
> Copyright © 1985 by Gretel Ehrlich. Reprinted by permission of Viking
> Penguin Inc.*

Now write a paragraph of your own patterned closely on the one above but including details and an illustration suitable to convey what it means to be a basketball player, a dancer, a journalist, a pianist, a mother, a father, a fast-food cook, a waiter, or a librarian.

3. Take notes for the next day or two on various ways that people use the words *weird* and *weirdo*. Then write a paragraph defining what these words mean today.

CHAPTER SUMMARY

In this chapter you've studied

- using definitions for clarity
- writing extended definitions
- defining through contrast
- finding details and examples to support topic sentences
- avoiding vague pronoun references
- achieving correct pronoun agreement

6

CHUNKY GUACAMOLE: ANALYTICAL WRITING

*A*nalysis involves looking closely at something and separating it into its various components (parts). An engine analysis, for example, includes testing the setting and condition of the points, spark plugs, carburetor, and timing—components of the engine's total performance. An analysis of a poem often shows how the images, structure, rhyme, and rhythm add up to get across the poem's theme. The samples of analytical writing we include here are vivid reviews, one of a Mexican restaurant and the other of an upscale bar/restaurant, both in the Midwest. As you read, you'll notice the lively word choice, fast pace, and strong tone of both reviews—although they're quite different.

HATS OFF! THREE CHEERS FOR OUR FAVORITE MEXICAN RESTAURANTS

Until late May, it was Lindo Mexico; now it's **Abril**—but whatever the name, this spacious, cheerful restaurant serves some of the better Mexican food in town. Burritos are so bountiful they nearly swallow the plate; tostadas suizas look

55

like a garden party; and the enormous concha could pass for a beach souvenir. When a dish says guacamole, the place doesn't skimp; and sour cream appears to be plopped from a ladle, not an eyedropper. Freshness, lavishness, and top quality are keys to our love affair with this premier Logan Square establishment.

We rate Abril's nachos—dripping with melted Chihuahua cheese, chunky guacamole, frijoles (refried beans), onions, tomatoes, and cilantro—the best ever. The chips crunch, cheese oozes, guacamole soothes, and cilantro zings, all at first bite. It's enough to make those ballpark impostors toss out their Cheez Whiz and repent.

Nearly as scrumptious is the "Mexican pizza," six soft, dainty flour tortillas layered with beans, chorizo (crumbly Mexican sausage), melted cheese, and a generous supply of freshly chopped tomatoes and onions. Served in soda glasses, the lime-festooned shrimp cocktail contains an abundance of firm little shrimp awash in a sweet-tart cocktail sauce dotted with diced avocado, tomatoes, onions, and cilantro.

Entrees range from tongue in tomato sauce to imaginative combinations, including one that partners a nacho with a flauta and a burrito. Most prices are in the five-to-six-dollar range.

There are six variations of burritos, each state-of-the-art. Go for the "gigante," which is a plate-dwarfing, crisply fried flour tortilla loaded with a thick, juicy filling of ground beef or chicken, frijoles, and rice, all smothered with guacamole, melted cheese, sour cream, green peppers and a bit too much tomato sauce.

Another showstopper is the concha, a delicate, crackly, deep-fried conch-shaped flour tortilla shell, generously laden with beans, spicy beef or chicken, guacamole, lettuce and tomato, and sour cream. Tostadas suizas carry nearly a head of shredded lettuce, under which are strips of moist chicken, beans, guacamole, and crisp corn tortillas. Flautas are excellent, with crunchy shells and plenty of guacamole and beef or chicken. More unusual is the enchilada filled with ham and melted cheese, and swathed with more of that good guacamole.

Margaritas are the icy, throat-numbing variety, and the pina colada comes decorated with a hefty slice of fresh pineapple. Service is pleasant and attentive; customers include a healthy mix of young people (many from the neighborhood), families, and older couples. Decorations abound, from colorful

murals to garlands of flourishing philodendron to a hand-
painted border of cacti and sombreros stretched across a
rooftop that resembles a hacienda. Slip a few coins into the
juke box, which contains an eclectic mix of Mexican love
songs, classical music, and big-band jazz, and settle back to
joyful gorging.

> —*Jill and Ron Rohde,* Chicago, *October 1985, p. 262. Reprinted with
> permission from* Chicago *magazine. Copyright © 1985 by WFMT, Inc.*

BABEL BLURS IRISH PUB

Have you ever noticed how ethnic restaurants wax and
wane in popularity? A few years ago we were suddenly
inundated with Mexican restaurants. Then came the Japanese
wave with sushi, sushi everywhere. Well, someone on Madison
Avenue decided that the Irish Pub/Grill was going to be the
next big thing, which spawned a whole bunch of "Irish"
franchises like Bennigan's.

Yet they forgot one thing—the Irish have no recognized
cuisine apart from potatoes, corned beef and cabbage. If the
Bennigans just stuck with the pub concept maybe they could
have mastered it, but they have far wider expectations—
which are sadly scattered.

This is a restaurant that doesn't believe in too much of a bad
thing. Every square inch of wall space is covered with motif in
extreme. Irish mixed with sports, mixed with movies. There are
boats hanging on the walls, along with tricycles, trumpets and
snowshoes—you name it, they nailed it up. Obviously the
management doubts the ability of its customers to entertain
themselves. The Al's Auction-o-rama theme gives folks something to talk about while they wait (and wait!) for service.

While we waited for our table, we sat at the bar and took an
informal poll of the patrons. None of them was Irish. And our
bartender was not the quintessential Irish one. In fact, he was
just this side of downright rude. Maybe that explains the lack of
Irish customers. Maybe the homemade potato chips really
explain it—at $2.00 a basket, the money would be better
spent on a bag of Ruffles.

Not surprisingly, the menu, like the decor, was all over the
road. Fettuccini Alfredo shared the menu with tostadas, crois-
sant sandwiches and Build-your-own-Burgers. And here's a

scary thought: Someone at this restaurant lies awake at night thinking up despicably cute names for all the entrees.

First we had "Steak 'n' a Clam," which amounted to Bennigan's version of the old surf and turf combination. The 8 oz. New York strip steak was cooked to order, but it was tough! The "clam" part was really clam sauce over a small portion of shrimp and overcooked linguini. It was no bargain at $9.95.

We had better luck on the next order, although we could barely keep a straight face while ordering. "The Veal Thing, Dahling!" was a high-priced 6 oz. veal cutlet ($12.95) sauteed in sherry butter with herbed rice, and it was *veal* tasty.

The house specialty for the evening was another Irish favorite, "Chicken Cacciatore," which was predictably bland. Hint: never order Italian food in an Irish restaurant.

Of course, we couldn't leave without sampling dessert. And we thought we would be safe by ordering cheesecake. As we expected, it was the frozen variety (which is not a crime in and of itself) but alas, it must have been a slow week for cheesecake, because it had that distinct "sittin' in the 'fridge" flavor.

Summary All in all, the food was mediocre, the service was slow, the decor was horrendous and the drinks were weak. And if the Bennigans are really Irish, then they are surely all out of luck.

—Laurie Dahlberg and Laurie Haag, unpublished review.
Reprinted by permission.

KEY ESSAY

You'll be doing your own restaurant review for this assignment. First, look again at the sample reviews, and answer these questions:

- What is the major concentration of the reviews? Food *service, customer*
- What do the reviewers write about other than food? *decor,*
- What qualities do the reviewers find important in the food?
  Freshness, Quantity, Appearance, Price – Taste

Reviews usually have very short paragraphs because they appear in newspapers and magazines, where essay-type paragraphs wouldn't give the readers' eyes enough breaks. Given the fact that the paragraphs must be brief, can you figure out why most of the paragraphs are divided as they are?

Now you're ready to try your hand as a reviewer. Choose a restaurant in your community or the nearest city—remember, you'll have to go there, with notebook in hand, to collect those lush details, even if you've been there before. Many restaurant reviewers like to invite friends along so they can sample more of the menu (and have more fun). You can report your friends' reactions as well as your own. Take plenty of notes, remembering to record elements other than food. From these notes, write a review designed for classmates that have never visited the place. Your review does not have to be positive: it can be negative or mixed. Imitate the samples here in length and informality. Concentrate on accurate and sensual description.

If you'd like to see more samples, look in food magazines like *Gourmet* and *Cuisine* and in most city newspapers, especially weekend issues. (Be aware, though, that newspaper editors usually discourage negative reviews.)

QUESTIONS FOR ANALYZING WRITING

After a good lunch, exchange your review with a classmate's. Read your partner's review and write the answers to these questions.

1. Do you get a clear idea of the writer's opinion of the restaurant? Do the details show you *why* that opinion came about?
2. Did the writer use enough descriptive language to appeal to your senses? Copy five of the descriptive phrases.
3. Other than food, what did the reviewer discuss? Are there any other things about the restaurant you'd like to know?
4. What did your partner do that you didn't in your review? What did you do that your partner didn't?

Read your partner's responses to see if you need to revise your review to make it complete and effective.

EXERCISES

SET A: WRITING FLUENTLY

1. An analysis similar to a review is a product analysis, or a buyer's report. Here's an example of one from *Consumer Reports*.

HOW HANDY IS THE HANDYMIXER?

A portable electric mixer is one of the handiest foodfixers around, and you can buy a good one for less than $20. Would a mixer that didn't trail an electrical cord be even handier? Black & Decker, with its $40 cordless Handymixer, is betting that the answer is yes.

The Handymixer is a lightweight, single-beater mixer that resembles a stubby hair dryer. Between uses the mixer sits in a charging base that is kept plugged in at all times. The base, which can sit on the counter or hang from the wall, holds the mixer, two whisks, a plastic stir paddle, and a beater.

Overall, the Handymixer did a good job on light tasks. It didn't complain when making instant pudding, cake mixes, mayonnaise, and milkshakes. Some quibbles: The Handymixer mayo was a little thinner than we are used to, and the milkshakes were left with some clumps of ice cream.

Although the Handymixer is clearly designed for light-duty tasks, we tried it on a few of the tougher jobs a portable mixer is sometimes called on to perform. The mixer sometimes labored when we made whipped cream or butter-cream frosting. Mashing potatoes and mixing cookie dough (tasks not mentioned in the mixer's instructions) were too much of a challenge. The mixer's beater tended to chase potato chunks around the bowl. Cookie dough slowed it to a crawl.

On a single charge, our units performed for about 35 minutes. That was long enough to whip through a series of tasks, from mixing cake batter to making mayonnaise, a milkshake, meringue and frosting. After an 18-hour recharge, our test samples ran for about 27 minutes—not quite enough to finish our series of tasks. But it's more than enough time to handle the mixing needed for a single main dish or dessert.

One of our three Handymixers died during our tests. We let it sit for six days without recharging, then put it to work. It stopped after only 19 minutes, and we couldn't revive it by plugging it into the charging base.

The Handymixer has two speeds: high and low. You must keep your finger on the switch constantly for low-speed operation. That was tiring on all but the shortest jobs. Otherwise, the mixer was comfortable and easy to hold, and only moderately noisy. The Handymixer wasn't particularly stable, though. When we set it down with its beater in place, it fell over at the slightest nudge.

Since the cord on a portable mixer has never bothered us, we are hard-pressed to imagine what singular advantage a cordless model yields. Black & Decker says the Handymixer is "a lot easier to use . . . especially . . . cooking over the stove." Easier still, we say, is stirring the pot with a spoon or a whisk.

—Copyright 1985 by Consumers Union of United States, Inc., Mount Vernon, N.Y. 10553. Reprinted by permission from Consumer Reports, *October 1985.*

Make a list of the aspects of the Handymixer that *Consumer Reports* covered. Is the review positive or negative? How do you know?

Choose a product that you own or use to write a consumer report about. Make up a list of the important aspects of this kind of product, and evaluate your own according to this list. Maybe these ideas will inspire you:

- your car
- your gun
- your running shoes
- your dogfood
- your shampoo or creme rinse
- your typewriter
- your pie crust mix
- your fishing rod
- your day-care center
- your thesaurus
- your word processing program
- your instant coffee

2. Another kind of consumer report compares and contrasts similar products. In this kind you also need a list of factors to judge the items by. For example, a comparison of three shampoos might include sections titled:

- Effectiveness in Cleaning
- Color and Smell
- Cost
- Conditioning Properties

When you write your comparative consumer report, you may even label the sections with these headings. The last section should be "Recommendations," in which you give overall advice to the consumer. You will not necessarily be wholeheartedly on the side of one of the products—for example, you might conclude, "Prell is a great choice for cleaning, but it will dry your hair out after a few uses. With Traite, your hair never feels squeaky clean, but its soft, supple condition will stay intact."

Use your friends as guinea pigs to help you collect the information you need to write your report.

For examples of comparative reviews, look at any *Consumer Reports* magazine. (The February 1985 issue reviews chocolate chip cookies.)

SET B: WRITING ACCURATELY

1. Study the following sentences. Write an explanation of what is the same about the placement of the comma in all of them. (Hint: Cover up the parts before the commas and read all the second parts aloud. Then reverse.)

a. Having put away a bundle of burritos and mountain of mole in our day, we admit to certain prejudices and particularities in assessing just what makes a top Mexican cafe.

b. Served in soda glasses, the lime-festooned shrimp cocktail contains an abundance of firm little shrimp.

c. One of several ostionerias (Mexican seafood houses) throughout the city, this dark, slightly foreboding spot is easily our favorite.

d. Besides loving snapper, we can always be persuaded to feast on camarones (shrimp).

e. Located between the Town Hall police station and some terrific vintage shops, Las Mananitas is a roomy storefront restaurant.

f. Attractively served in volcanic stone mortar, the guacamole is smooth, thick, and amply perfumed with fresh lime juice.

g. At lunch, there's often a wholesome, freshly prepared chicken soup.

h. On bustling 47th Street, Elvia's is more a snack shop than a full-fledged restaurant.

i. On our original visit, several years ago, a customer from a nearby table sat down with us and ended up inviting us to his home for Easter.

j. When a dish says guacamole, the place doesn't skimp.

k. Although nearly every entree is exemplary, the real star is huachinango (red snapper).

l. If only the chips were less greasy, perfection would be at hand.

m. If the food isn't quite spicy enough, a side dish of marinated hot peppers, carrots, and onions provides all the fire needed.

n. Though Tacos & Things can be noisy and occasionally confused when crowded, we'll always be seduced by its carnival-like charm and relaxed, friendly atmosphere.

o. Although the enchilada potosina doesn't look like much, this humble corn tortilla dipped in red sauce and filled with onion-sparked anejo cheese offers a mellow and satisfying flavor.

p. Because the prices are so high, we only sampled one appetizer.

q. After we finished our soup and salad, we were almost too full for the main course.

Now, can you express what the difference is between sentences *a* through *i* and sentences *j* through *q*?

Fill in the beginnings of the following sentences in any way similar to examples *a* through *q*.

r. _____, we sampled the lobster tail.

s. _____, creamy hot fudge pooled in the dish.

t. _____, finally the cheeseburgers arrived.

u. _____, the chapatas disappointed us.

v. _____, crispy fried chicken is Sarah's favorite.

w. _____, Mark will only eat salad.

2. Fill in commas needed in the following paragraph. Some places need commas in series (see Chapter 1), and some need commas after introductory elements. Some sentences need no commas.

My sister Kay and I are only a year apart. When we were teenagers we were very close. We often conspired to fool my parents. Once we told them that we were going camping. Instead of lying awake being scared of night sounds Kay and I stayed out in the city all night. We went to Barney's Burgers The Gallery and The Metropole. We ended up in the Pussycat Club at four in the morning. Flirting drinking and dancing filled our evening instead of peaceful stargazing. Thinking we'd never get caught we sneaked into our home early in the morning. In our excitement about our clever trick we forgot to get our stories lined up. When my mother asked about our camping trip Kay and I separately told totally made-up completely vivid and utterly contradictory stories.

3. Combine each of the following groups of short sentences into a long sentence, using commas when appropriate. Add and take out words as needed.

a. My wife and I make bets.
We bet on little things.
We bet on whether she'll be late for work.
We bet on whether I'll get an A on a test.
We bet on what the temperature outside is.

b. Sometimes we bet five dollars.
Sometimes we bet a Chinese dinner.
One of us may not be sure of his or her side of the bet.
Then the one who is unsure may offer only a nickel bet.

c. We both work.
We share our money.
The bets are meaningless.
They are fun.

d. It was below zero outside yesterday.
My wife said it was above zero.
Tonight she is taking me to the House of Hunan.

SET C: WRITING LOGICALLY AND COHERENTLY

1. Classify the restaurants in your area into categories that would help a newcomer to the community. Write the restaurants in lists according to category. Then write one sentence under each restaurant to give the newcomer a general idea of what it's like.

2. Write a list of questions that will make a good survey of people's opinions about a popular fast-food restaurant. Exchange your list with other students' lists so you can add important questions you forgot. Using your list, interview three to five people who have been to this restaurant and take notes on their responses.

3. Using your interview notes, write a review of the fast-food restaurant. Incorporate ideas and quotations from each of your interviewees. After you write the review once, rethink the order of your points. Ask yourself whether there is a more effective or emphatic organization.

CHAPTER SUMMARY

In this chapter you've studied

- analyzing the attributes of a restaurant and a product
- writing a descriptive, complete review
- reading another writer's review for completeness and vividness
- writing a detailed, organized consumer report
- using commas after introductory elements in a sentence

Ship

GOOD LAND, GOOD LIVING, AND GOOD BOURBON: LEARNING TO SUMMARIZE

Sooner or later you will need to use someone else's writing to support and develop the ideas in a paper of your own. Your days of copying the "Witchcraft" entry out of the encyclopedia are definitely over. Learning how to summarize another person's written ideas—accurately and in your own words—is both difficult and valuable. To illustrate, we are reprinting an informal essay about highways by Russell Baker and offering a sample 125-word summary. Then we will ask you to summarize another essay by Baker.

VOCABULARY

drudgery	boring, unpleasant task
hurtle	move with great speed
stupor	dazed or drugged condition
grandeur	greatness, splendor
squalor	filth and misery
entrepreneur	businessman
exasperating	irritating
hamlets	small villages

GOD'S OWN COUNTRY

Louisville, KY, *August, 1962*—They have an exciting new idea in highway engineering out here. It is called the low-speed, two-lane, unlimited access road, and to anyone who dreads the drudgery of expressway driving it looks like the wave of the future.

For one thing, it is more dangerous than the old-fashioned superhighway. Farmers are forever pulling out of cornfields right across the traveler's bow, and hairpin curves are constantly threatening to send him to Kingdom Come. Giant tractor rigs hurtle past within inches, smacking the car with a shock wave that leaves it shuddering. All this not only appeals to the natural American love of excitement, but also keeps the driver from sinking into the drowsing stupor that makes turnpike driving such a trial.

The real beauty of the low-speed, two-lane, unlimited access road, however, is that it has character, individuality and style that tell the traveler a little something of the variety of America. This is what the superhighways have lost. Except for minor differences in vegetation the New Jersey Turnpike looks exactly like Florida's Sunshine State Parkway, which looks like the Maine Turnpike, which looks like Interstate 95 in New Hampshire, Virginia and North Carolina.

The superhighway is designed for a nation of bypassers. It bypasses the grandeur of Frenchman's Bay, bypasses the magnificence of New York City, bypasses the sprawl of Philadelphia, bypasses the neon of the Florida Gold Coast. When the Federal Interstate Highway System is completed, it will be possible to bypass all of America.

The motorist who is bypassing his country may get to his destination a little faster, but he becomes a traveler who is untraveled. Instead of becoming a richer man, he is reduced to a dozing lump of boredom whose horizon is no broader than the next "rest stop."

. . . This is a good country to examine at slow cruising speed. There is, for example, the sharp shift in moods that occurs at the Big Sandy River where Route 60 crosses from West Virginia into Kentucky. Behind, to the east, lie the industrial towns of Huntington and Charleston, the steamy summer air of clusters of railroad shops and the ammoniac smell of chemical plants. Back further still to the east lie the breathtaking Appalachian peaks and river valleys. The traveler whose preconceptions have readied him to find West Virginia a place of poverty and squalor is shocked to find that it is also a place of Swiss beauty and much industrial promotion.

Then, swooping up into the hills of eastern Kentucky, the mood of the road shifts abruptly. Bypassing nothing, it allows time to read the changes in roadside signs. (Another charming feature of the two-lane road is that signs are posted everywhere to relieve the monotony of the landscape.)

In Virginia the billboards reveal a sharp competitive instinct among cave operators. "World's Only Known Anthodites," boasts a typical cave entrepreneur outside Front Royal. In West Virginia they betray an up-and-at-'em mood. "We Feature the Future," declares the welcome billboard at Ceredo, W. Va. And in eastern Kentucky they announce the beginning of the Bible Belt. . . .

Winding westward past the country of crude, unpainted shacks and small tobacco plots, the road flows into the lusher farmland of Shelby County. "Shelby County: Home of Good People, Good Land and Good Living," reads the welcoming sign. And as it moves toward Lexington through the Blue Grass country, the evidence of good land and good living and billboards selling good bourbon tell the tourist how the country around him is changing as he moves west.

For incurable bypassers, it is an exasperating road, full of ill-graded curves, and farmers moving at stately pace and red lights stopping progress in unbypassed hamlets. For those who can take their bypasses or leave them alone, it is a cheering reminder that this is still a country that remains to be discovered by those with the will to explore.

— *"God's Own Country" from* No Cause for Panic *by Russell Baker (J. B. Lippincott), pp. 87–89, 1962. Copyright © 1962, 1963, 1964 by The New York Times Company. Reprinted by permission of Harper & Row, Publishers, Inc.*

SAMPLE SUMMARY

The "low-speed, two-lane, unlimited access road" is more dangerous than an expressway, but it is also more exciting and won't let a driver go to sleep. More important, the individual differences among two-lane roads encourage a traveler to notice the variety of the scenery. Turnpikes, parkways, and interstates all look alike. They also bypass the most interesting parts of the journey: expressway travelers save time but don't see much. Moving slowly on a two-lane road, drivers experience sights and smells up close. They can also read the billboards, which reveal local atmosphere and chart the travelers' progress. Two-lane highways frustrate drivers in a hurry, but people who don't want to bypass everything can explore America on these roads. [125 words]

KEY ESSAY

Your writing assignment for this chapter is to summarize the following essay by Russell Baker:

MORE TO BE PITIED THAN FEARED

On the occasion of Halloween, let a good word be said for monsters. For Frankenstein's luckless electrified oaf. For Count Dracula in that uncomfortable winged collar. For the Wolf Man and his son, and for King Kong and his son, and for all the poor mummies dug out of Egypt.

They have never been properly understood, principally because of publicity agents and psychologists. The publicity agents always depicted them as horrors, and the psychologists warn against letting the children become too involved with them. Both views are wrong.

The common trait of all the really great monsters is their touching human simplicity. This is probably why they have endured so well and why they are so popular with children today. In most cases, they are simple romantics driven to distraction and then to violence by a human society which will not leave them in peace.

In the typical monster film, the truly monstrous deeds are done by the respectable citizenry against the monster. By urbane scientists working on the principle that anything goes in the quest for knowledge. By panicked lynch mobs of townspeople. By aggressive businessmen—as in King Kong—who mean to get rich at the monster's expense.

Consider the Frankenstein case. Here we have a gentle imbecile who likes to smoke cigars and hear the violin. He yearns for the simple life, but it is denied him by the bumbling scientist who created him and by an incompetent (and probably underpaid) lab technician.

They have stupidly outfitted the wretched fellow with a third-rate brain. Not content with that, they have left electrodes sticking out of his neck and have dressed him in a comically undersized suit. The thing goes out in search of friendship only to discover that there is nothing society fears and hates like a misfit.

Before long the bloodhounds are after him. The poor devil is wreaking havoc in his pathetic attempts to get away, and the mob destroys him. It is a parable of sorts about the nuclear age.

Count Dracula is a more complex case. Superficially, there seems little to be said for him. And yet he is basically a victim of misfortune. Something bit him; consequently, he cannot entirely die. He needs blood to eke out a drab existence which requires him to spend the sunlight hours in a coffin.

It quickly becomes apparent to the group of stuffed shirts entertaining him that he is a desperate case. But does the doctor offer to treat him at the blood bank? No.

Instead, he torments the Count with wolfsbane and mirrors. The Count is fighting for his life, and the doctor sneaks upon him at sleep and puts a stake in his heart. Is there a hidden comment here on medical care for the luckless?

The Wolf Man has much the same problem. Most of the time he is sweet, genial Lon Chaney, Jr., but when the moon is full he grows face hair and becomes quite mad, due to an unfortunate old werewolf bite. The condition is pitiable, but in movie after movie Chaney is invariably shot by some colorless leading man to protect society against its unfortunates.

And Kong. Poor Kong. His need is the love of a good woman. His love is unrequited. He is too ugly. In the end, the whole weight of the Pentagon is brought down upon him as the Air Force guns him off the Empire State Building. So much for lovesick freaks.

The mummies also seek love. Usually they have been buried alive for several thousands of years and are dug up for the titillation of science. Naturally, their thoughts turn at once to women. Naturally the women are repelled. (Mummies lack all the social graces.) And society does the outcast in.

And so it always is with the monsters. They are not quite tragic figures, but only noble unfortunates. They are not terrifying, but only pitiable. If the children like them, it may be comforting evidence that the children can still pity.

May the monsters find society hospitable and good women romantic this Halloween.

> — *"More to Be Pitied Than Feared" from* No Cause for Panic *by Russell Baker (J. B. Lippincott), pp. 186–188. Copyright © 1962, 1963, 1964 by The New York Times Company. Reprinted by permission of Harper & Row, Publishers, Inc.*

Before you begin to write your summary of this essay, study the following guidelines. They should help you in learning how to make accurate, useful summaries of other people's ideas:

1. Be sure that you understand the material: look up unfamiliar words and reread difficult sentences.
2. Stick to main ideas; leave out details that merely expand or illustrate major points.
3. Pay attention to paragraph changes, which usually signal another main point.
4. Don't introduce your own views or make comments about the material.
5. Don't change the tone or attitude of the original.
6. Keep ideas in the same order as the original.
7. Express the ideas in your own words; use quotation marks when you borrow phrases directly from the original.

Now write your summary of "More To Be Pitied Than Feared." Try to limit your summary to no more than 150 words, if possible.

QUESTIONS FOR ANALYZING WRITING

Apart from brevity, the criteria for judging a summary involve three goals: including all important points, eliminating all unnecessary details, and avoiding any irrelevant additions. Trade papers with some other student in the class, and study your classmate's summary by comparing it with the original essay. Then answer these questions in writing, being as specific and detailed as you can in your responses:

1. Have all important points been included?
2. Are there unnecessary details to cut?
3. Are there irrelevant additions to eliminate?
4. Does the summary catch the tone and attitude of the original?

When you get your own paper back, edit it according to your partner's instructions. Write in points which you had overlooked; cross out any words, phrases, or sentences that need to go.

EXERCISES

SET A: WRITING FLUENTLY

1. Read the following short passages and then write a two-sentence summary of each passage:

> There exists a mistaken idea that manners are more important for women than for men. Wrongheaded ideas about what constitutes masculinity cause some men to adopt deliberate attitudes of rudeness. There is nothing appealing, however, about a man who is loud, brusque, unsympathetic, cruel, or domineering. These are not masculine qualities; they are brutish ones. Manners and masculinity go together. Parents who equate good manners with "sissy" behavior are in large part responsible for this male attitude toward manners. A boy who grows up thinking that rudeness is "manly" will have placed an unnecessary obstacle between himself and other people.
>
> —*From* Is Your Volkswagon a Sex Symbol*? by Jean Rosenbaum, M.D.*
> *Copyright © 1972 by Jean Rosenbaum. A Hawthorn book. Reprinted by*
> *permission of E. P. Dutton, a division of New American Library.*

> X-rays are taken of over half the population each year. They're used by dentists to check for impacted teeth, jaw fractures, and tooth alignment and by doctors to diagnose everything from tumors to tuberculosis to heart disease. No one disputes that, since their discovery in 1895, x-rays have saved millions of lives ... nor that all radiation involves an

element of risk. Which side of the x-ray debate you come down on depends on just how much risk you perceive.

—Elaine Dutka, "X-Rays: The Inside Picture," Cosmopolitan, *May 1981, 104*

With its striking imagery, deft choreography, bright colors and quick cuts, music video has attracted a huge audience. It's also caused an angry stir, albeit a confused one: assessments of its impact are highly subjective, with anecdotes available to support any point of view. And it may simply be impossible to sort out the effects of music videos from network programming, not to mention other social phenomena. So take your choice: "Children are being bombarded with messages of violence and sexuality that are very confusing and suggest easy ways out of complex problems," says Dr. Eli Newberger, director of family-development study at Children's Hospital in Boston. "For any kids who are reasonably put together, it doesn't drive them into anything," counters David Elkind, a professor of child study at Tufts University. "Nobody knows exactly what MTV is doing to us," suggests Robert Jay Lifton, the author of numerous studies on violence, who is now a professor at John Jay College of Criminal Justice in New York.

—Eric Gelman with Mark Starr, Lynda Wright, Monroe Anderson, Ginny Carroll, "MTV's Message," Newsweek, *30 December 1985, p. 54.*

2. It's difficult to summarize someone else's ideas. Can you do any better with your own writing? Look over the key essays you've written for this class, especially those for Chapters 2, 4, and 5. Choose one and try to sum up your main points in fifty words or less.

3. Select an important passage from a textbook that you use in one of your other classes this semester. Choose something you think you need to know and remember. The passage doesn't have to be very long—two or three paragraphs will do. After rereading it carefully, write a summary of the main points in the passage. Include a photocopy of the passage with your summary. Perhaps completing this assignment will convince you that summarizing material in your own words is a good way to learn and remember information that you need to know. Try this technique in studying for all your classes.

SET B: WRITING ACCURATELY

1. Pronouns allow us to avoid repetition and help us to keep our sentences and ideas unified. One reason why pronouns are so useful is that they come in different forms, which convey different grammatical meanings: singular or plural, masculine or feminine or neuter, subject or object. Here is a list of personal pronouns: we, they, her, it, I, him, them, us, me, he, you, she. From this list, fill in the following blank using as many different ones as sound right:

● _____ hit the ball.

Now shift the same "person" to a different position in the sentence and fill in the pronouns that fit:

● The ball hit _____.

Are there any pronouns that can go in both slots? Which pronouns can you put in this blank?

● Luis threw the ball at _____.

Write sentences in which you correctly use all of the *subject pronouns* (those that fit in the first sentence above): I, you, he, she, it, we, they. Use each pronoun at least once. Then write sentences in which you correctly use all of the *object pronouns* (those that fit in the second and third sentences): me, you, him, her, it, us, them. You may be able to use more than one pronoun in a sentence.

2. You may have trouble with the form of pronouns in only a few situations. One is when you have a compound subject or object. (*Compound* means more than one item, usually linked with *and* or some other connecting word.) Here are two compounds which involve pronouns:

● *Carlos and I* once trapped a snake; then we argued about whether it belonged to *him or me*.

You can check to see if you have the right form by blocking out one item from the pair:

● [Carlos and] *I* once trapped a snake; then we argued about whether it belonged to [him or] *me*.

The following exercises should help you to get a feel for using the correct pronouns in compounds.

A. Step 1. Write three sentences using the following pattern:

● *The* + first noun + verb + second noun + *to* (or *for*) + third noun.

Sample:

● The teacher demonstrated the technique for the class.
    (noun 1)   (verb)   (noun 2)   (noun 3)

Step 2. Add a pronoun to the first noun in each sentence:

● *She and* the teacher demonstrated the technique for the class.

Step 3. Add a pronoun to the third noun of each sentence:

● The teacher demonstrated the technique for the class *and (I or me?).*

B. Fill in each of the blanks in the following sentences with the correct form of the pronoun:

1. (He, Him) _____ and his coach need to find a way to communicate more effectively.
2. Please send the test results to both the counselor and (I, me) _____.
3. Jack and (I, me) _____ are going to enter the breakdance contest.
4. The deal must guarantee profits for (he, him) _____ and his partner.
5. (She, Her) _____ and her group pressured the council for months.
6. The council was pressured for months by (she, her) _____ and her group.

3. Fill in these blanks with pronouns that refer to yourself (I, me, my, or mine):

● Marshall is taller than _____.

- My aunt seems to like you more than _____.
- _____ winning the lottery delighted us all.
- My parents approve of _____ going away to school.

These sentences present some unusual uses of the language. The first two involve words that have been left out. If you put the omitted words back in the sentences, you can tell which pronoun is called for:

- Marshall is taller than *I* am (tall).
- My aunt seems to like you more than *I* like you.
              or
- My aunt seems to like you more than she likes *me*.

In the second instance, the choice of pronouns obviously changes the meaning of the sentence, which becomes clear when you fill in the omitted words.
    The other pair of sentences above involve close attention to the precise meaning of the words:

- *My* winning the lottery delighted us all.
              that is
    We were all delighted by my act of winning, not by me.
- My parents approve of *my* going away to school.
              that is
    My parents approve of my going, not necessarily of me.

    In this second example you might have chosen *me* because you are used to hearing the object form after a phrase like "approve of." Using a pronoun correctly depends on understanding it in relation to the words around it. In both of the examples we have just considered, the use of the possessive form (*my*) makes the meaning clear. The rule is, then, that when you use a pronoun before an -*ing* word, you usually use the possessive pronoun form: my, your, his, her, its, our, their. However, you have to be careful because there are times when the meaning will call for a different form of the pronoun:

- We caught a glimpse of *them* running through the woods.

    What did we catch a glimpse of? Of them, not their running —they just happened to be running when we saw them.

The following paragraph contains some of the errors that writers make with pronoun forms. Some of the forms are correct, some are not. On a separate sheet rewrite the paragraph, changing the incorrect forms to correct ones. Underline the words that you changed.

> For his twelfth birthday Ronnie Moran's father let him invite two friends to go to the Bears' game with Ronnie and his dad. Ronnie chose Oliver and I. When we got to the stadium Ronnie sat with his dad, and Oliver and me sat across the aisle. But Oliver complained that a tall man interfered with him seeing the field, so he switched seats with Mr. Moran, who's not much taller than me. Both me and him had to stretch to see over the man in front; but as soon as the game started, we forgot about us having to strain and got caught up in the action on the playing field. One of my favorite players, Walter Payton, was playing that day, and I was thrilled to see him running down the field in person.

SET C: WRITING LOGICALLY AND COHERENTLY

1. Write a one-page explanation of why it is all right for children to watch monster movies. Use several points from the summary you made of Russell Baker's essay. When you include a summarized idea from Baker, be sure to credit him and connect his points to yours, using phrases like these:

- As Russell Baker points out . . .
- According to Russell Baker . . .
- Monsters, as Baker says, are . . .

If you actually use any of Baker's phrases, be sure to put those in quotation marks.

2. Rewrite the last two paragraphs of "More To Be Pitied Than Feared." Use the same number of sentences Baker does and make all the points he makes, but state them in your own words. This kind of rewrite is called a *paraphrase*, and it will show you how to arrange and develop a conclusion in the same way a professional writer does.

CHAPTER SUMMARY

In this chapter you've studied

- summarizing an essay
- editing another student's summary
- using pronouns effectively and accurately
- using summarized ideas to support explanations
- paraphrasing

8

AT THE MOVIES: REPORTING OPINIONS

When you have to spend at least five dollars for a movie ticket these days, you want to get your money's worth. You'd like to know something about the film, and you'd probably like to know what somebody else thought about it. But not everybody likes the same movie, or even the same kind of movie. The following reviews offer differing opinions about a major motion picture. After you have read them, we will ask you to make your own judgment about this film.

The first review comes from *Time* magazine. We've shortened it a little, and our cuts are indicated by ellipsis dots (three periods). Here is some vocabulary to help you read the review more easily:

VOCABULARY

indulgence	yielding to desires
redress	set right, remedy
sunder	break apart, divide
remobilize	recover and prepare for an emergency

repress	hold back
disintegration	falling apart
straitened	restricted, difficult

Look up any other words you are not sure about.

BREAKUP

Infidelity in the movies ... is seen as a mostly middle-class affliction.... The indulgences that are paid for in painful scenes and sleepless nights are usually denied the working class.

Twice in a Lifetime would deserve respectful attention if all it did were redress that imbalance. But the story of how the 30-year marriage of steelworker Harry Mackenzie (Gene Hackman ...) and his wife Kate (Ellen Burstyn) sunders has another dimension....

To the filmmakers, the disintegration of a marriage is not at all an occasion for faultfinding or for a highly compressed dramatic crisis. Everyone in *Twice in a Lifetime* is decent. Harry only reluctantly concedes the validity of his need for emotional renewal, and he never entirely forgives himself the pain he causes. He is, in fact, as surprised as everyone when, while celebrating his 50th birthday with his fellow mill hands, he falls passionately in love with a barmaid (Ann-Margret). Stunned, Kate is tempted toward but fights off a state of permanent victimization. Helping her to remobilize are a married daughter (Amy Madigan), who ferociously expresses the anger her mother represses, and a younger sibling (Ally Sheedy), whose wedding, in suddenly straitened circumstances, requires some ingenuity from all three women.

Family dramas are always an invitation to fine ensemble acting, and these players are up to it.... Only Ann-Margret is somewhat shortchanged by the script: her motives are never made fully clear. Sometimes, too, the movie feels overly tidy and pleased with its own humanism. But it unashamedly keeps scratching away at small behavioral truths, and draws some blood in the process.

—*Richard Schickel,* Time, *18 November 1985, 92. Copyright © 1985.
Time, Inc. All rights reserved. Reprinted by permission from* Time.

Here is another view, this one taken from *The New Republic,* magazine.

VOCABULARY

milieu	environment, surroundings
confrontation	meeting head on
contend	state, assert

NOT THE SAME

Twice in a Lifetime. What do they mean twice? Do they think this is only the second time we've seen this picture? A married man, with wife and children and grandchildren, turns 50, goes to his birthday party, and there meets a woman somewhat younger and sexier than his wife.

This time he's a steel-mill worker, played by Gene Hackman, the place is Seattle, and the milieu is comfortable working class. The wife is Ellen Burstyn, doing her best to be a Good Wife, aware that hubby is a bit removed, trying to bring him back with Good Wifery. The other woman is hard to care about because she makes such a strong, deliberate play for the married man, with no thought of anyone else; and the trouble is compounded because she is played by Ann-Margret, a disadvantage.

After all the utterly familiar exchanges and scenes, we are left with what is supposed to be a confrontation of truth. A marriage can wither, can simply wear out, like a pair of shoes. What the film omits in its truth-baring is that, in this case, it hasn't played out for the wife, only for the husband. What it also omits is that in our society, when only one of the 50-year-old partners in a marriage decides that it's over, it's usually the husband; and this has a lot to do with the fact that, in our society, he has a better chance with younger women than the wife has with younger men. At the end of the picture Burstyn has a new hairdo and new clothes but not exactly the same fresh chance that Hackman has. . . .

—*Stanley Kauffmann,* The New Republic, *18 November 1985, 28–29.*
Reprinted by permission of The New Republic, *copyright © 1985,*
The New Republic, Inc.

KEY ESSAY

Do you think you would like to see *Twice in a Lifetime*? Imagine that a group of fellow students wants to know whether or not to rent this movie for a public screening to benefit their organization. They are considering several choices, and they ask you about *Twice in a Lifetime*. Although you may not have seen the film, you have read these reviews. Write a report in which you describe the movie and summarize the reviewers' opinions. Your report should be made in three parts:

4-paragraphs

1. **Background**: state who is in the movie and give a brief summary of the plot.
2. **Details**: explain what the reviewers liked and did not like about the film. You may divide this section in two—one paragraph for positive comments and another for negative criticisms, or one paragraph for each review.
3. **Recommendation(s)**: make a recommendation to the group based on your reaction to and evaluation of the two reviews.

In reporting on these reviews you may want to quote briefly from them. If you do, follow these examples:

- According to Richard Schickel, the movie is sometimes "overly tidy" but "unashamedly keeps scratching away at small behavioral truths."
- Both reviewers think the part of the "other woman" is weak. Stanley Kauffmann doesn't like her because "she makes such a strong, deliberate play for the married man" without thinking about the other people involved.

QUESTIONS FOR ANALYZING WRITING

Get together with someone else in the class and read your papers aloud to each other. As you read, pay attention to any places that you stumble over: put a mark in the margin so that you can check these places out later. As you listen to your partner, concentrate on phrases and sentences that are not completely clear. Exchange papers and look for the rough places that you heard in your partner's writing. Ask yourself these questions about your partner's paper:

1. Are there any words or phrases that need to be changed or cut?
2. Are quotations smoothly incorporated into the rest of the text?
3. Can some sentences be smoothed out by rearranging or rewriting the words?
4. Which sentences describe the movie most effectively?

Write down at least two suggestions for your partner to consider. For example, you might write: "The first quotation in the second paragraph isn't clearly connected to the sentences around it" or "I don't understand what you mean by the phrase 'family-type entertainment' in the first sentence of your conclusion." Also make two comments about parts of the essay that are well written: for example, you might write, "Your definition of unnecessary violence was especially clear."

Get your paper back and revise those questionable sentences that your reading and your partner's suggestions pointed out.

EXERCISES

SET A: WRITING FLUENTLY

Fun

1. Write a one-page description of the perfect movie, the movie that you've always wanted Hollywood to make. Tell who would be in it, and give a detailed account of the story. Describe any other parts of the movie—setting, music, special effects—that you think would be important.

2. Read the following review of a television show, and write a summary of the main criticisms in your own words (no direct quotations). The review is 315 words long; try to make your summary no more than 160 words long.

> [*Night Heat*] is notable chiefly for its overacting and its single-minded dedication to vintage cop-show cliches. The heroes are true-blue. The heavies have absolutely no redeeming qualities. . . .

Were it not for the credits at the end, we'd swear on a stack of *Naked City* scripts that this...effort is written by a not-too-sophisticated computer that suffers memory lapses. Thus unexplained characters bob up to provide information the police badly need if they're going to find the baddie. Then the strange characters vanish, never to be heard from again....

The name [*Night Heat*] is also the title of a newspaper column by Tom Kirkwood (played by Allan Royal), who spends most of his time with—and gets most of his column material from—two policemen, either at the precinct house or a local bar. It is through his eyes, and comments, that we learn about "the problems and rewards of working the night shift on a major metropolitan police force."

The two protagonists are detectives Kevin O'Brien (Scott Hylands), the knowledgeable veteran, and Frank Giambone (Jeff Wincott), the impetuous youngster. They do a credible job. It's usually the criminals who act like raving maniacs....

Plots? Consider a series of presumably accidental deaths that turn out to be the work of a Federal narcotics agent knocking off his undercover team so he can cash in on a big drug buy they made. Consider a holdup man being captured and his brother deciding to free him by holding the entire precinct house hostage. Consider Detective Giambone's old girl friend, now an actress, getting mixed up with a big-time drug dealer who kills people by mixing potassium cyanide with their cocaine. Go ahead, consider, We've seen them, and when they're stretched out to an hour, with cello suspense music going on and on to help fill the time between all those late-night commercials, they can be considerably less than entertaining.

—Don Merrill, "Night Heat Review," from TV Guide, 30 November 1985, p. 1. Reprinted with permission from TV GUIDE® Magazine. Copyright © 1985 by Triangle Publications, Inc. Radnor, Pennsylvania.

3. As the manager of the school film series, you have to write concise summaries of the movies you are showing. Your descriptions of the films are the primary means of attracting your potential audience, and the continued funding of your program depends on good attendance. These promotional previews appear in the school newspaper, and you are limited to ninety words. Pick any movie that you know well and describe it in a way that will bring students in.

For Friday/Monday

SET B: WRITING ACCURATELY   *Do!*   TENSE

1. In summarizing a plot or telling about an event as if it is happening now, writers often use what is called the *historical present tense*:

- The gladiator *enters* the arena; all eyes *are* on him as he *bows* to the emperor.

Although these events clearly occurred in the past, the writer keeps them alive and immediate by using present tense, but this strategy works only when there is no chance for confusion. We often encounter the historical present tense in writings about movies and books because they continue to exist, even though our experiences with them may be over.

Both of the movie reviews that you read at the start of this chapter are written in the present tense:

- Harry only reluctantly *concedes* the validity of his need for emotional renewal, and he never entirely *forgives* himself the pain he *causes*.

Tense refers to the time—past, present, future—that is indicated by the verbs the writer uses. If Richard Schickel had written his review in past tense, the above sentence would have read this way:

- Harry only reluctantly *conceded* the validity of his need for emotional renewal, and he never entirely *forgave* himself the pain he *caused*.

As you can see, the past tense is most often indicated by adding *-ed* to the present tense (concede ⟶ conceded, cause ⟶ caused) or by changing a vowel in the middle of the verb (forgive ⟶ forgave).

It is important to know what tense you are writing in and to be consistent: if you change tense for no reason or without realizing that you have, this shift will confuse your readers.

The following passage mixes present and past tenses. Rewrite the paragraph, and put all the verbs into the present tense.

Do For

Spenser: For Hire is based on the detective novels of Robert Parker and is several steps above the average television crime

Friday / Monday

series. It is well acted and well worth watching. Robert Ulrich proved that he is an excellent actor in the part of the tough, well-read private investigator Spenser. He was believable when he fought the bad guys, and he is believable when he quotes Shakespeare. But when the script called for him to be cute and kittenish with his girl friend, Susan, he is not believable. A cute Spenser was simply embarrassing. In the books Spenser and Susan tease and traded playful insults, but they are not kittenish. The TV show needed to fix that part of their relationship.

Read

2. You probably don't use the *semicolon* very often in your writing, but it is a useful mark of punctuation. You can use the semicolon like a weak period; you can also use it like a strong comma. In the sentence you just read the semicolon acted as a stop sign; it told you that you had reached the end of one idea and would go on to a related idea in the second part of the sentence. Here is another example:

- This scientist tries to predict earthquakes; she is working to improve her accuracy.

Such sentences are called *compound sentences*; they are made up of two or more simple sentences. In these sentences the semicolon is functioning much like a period; it separates two full sentences that are closely related. You could also put a connecting word (and, but, or, nor, for, yet, so) between the two sentences, but then you would use a comma instead of a semicolon:

- This scientist tries to predict earthquakes, and she is working to improve her accuracy.

Sometimes the two simple sentences in a compound sentence already contain some commas; so you use a semicolon as a strong comma, to mark the important separation between the two related ideas. The sentence you just read illustrates this use of a semicolon. Here is another example, taken from Stanley Kauffmann's review of *Twice in a Lifetime*:

> The other woman is hard to care about because she makes such a strong, deliberate play for the married man, with no thought of anyone else; and the trouble is compounded because she is played by Ann-Margret, a disadvantage.

Kauffmann punctuates another compound sentence with a semicolon. Can you find the second example? Do you see why he uses a semicolon?

Here are some sentences to complete. We have supplied the beginning or ending sentence of a compound that needs a semicolon; you should write the other sentence.

a. Scare tactics don't seem to work on most smokers; _____ _____.

b. _____; every nine-teen minutes an American is killed with a handgun.

c. The defendants' supporters circulated petitions, filed legal appeals, and picketed the governor's mansion; but _____ _____.

d. _____; and the students still didn't understand the assignment.

e. When a man raises his voice, he's being forceful; _____ _____.

3. The *colon* is an economical way to signal to your reader that more information is on its way. This additional material may come in several forms:

A STATEMENT THAT EXPLAINS:

- "Only Ann-Margret is somewhat shortchanged by the script: her motives are never made fully clear."

A STATEMENT THAT ILLUSTRATES:

- Epilepsy was once considered a mark of honor: in ancient Rome epileptics were given high government offices.

A SINGLE WORD OR SERIES THAT AMPLIFIES
A GENERAL WORD OR PHRASE:

- The strangest thing about Uncle Fred is his car: a battered old Chevy.
- We always came back from Grandma's with lots of goodies: peanut brittle, chewing gum, plastic toys, homemade cookies, and little bars of scented soap.

Notice that in the preceding sentences, the colon follows a complete sentence. You don't need a colon between a verb and the rest of the sentence:

- My most difficult classes are psychology, physics, and conversational Greek. (no colon)

A. Combine the following sentences by using colons and eliminating repetitious or unnecessary words:

1. A well-disciplined runner's daily practice has three important parts. They are the warm-up exercises, the run itself, and the wind-down.
2. The public outcry and the numerous protests did no good. The Rosenbergs were executed in June of 1953 for espionage.
3. My parents saved an unbelievable collection of useless mementos. They saved toys, report cards, worn-out sneakers, concert programs, and prom dresses.
4. We can express ourselves without words in all sorts of ways. We can lift an eyebrow, make a face, or change the tone of our voice to convey our nonverbal meanings.

B. Using a holiday as your subject, write two complete sentences that can be joined by a colon.

C. In a complete sentence, list at least three performers who are popular because of unusual appearance. Use a colon to supply their names.

SET C: WRITING LOGICALLY AND COHERENTLY

1. Write a page describing the plot of a movie or TV show you've seen recently. Use present tense all the way through, as the movie reviewers do in the two reviews at the beginning of this chapter. If you are unsure about the use of present tense or how to describe a plot, look at the sample reviews again.

2. Here are excerpts from two more reviews of *Twice in a Lifetime*. One supports the positive view of the film; the other expresses a negative opinion. After you have read these reviews, summarize the points that each makes about the movie. Write a paragraph for each review. Then write a third paragraph in which

you explain why the two reviewers disagree and which opinion you find more convincing.

> *Twice in a Lifetime* doesn't work its magic by breaking any new ground; it does so with simplicity, honesty and fault- less performances. Once past the sentimental exposition, the film moves into a series of penetrating slices-of-life, from Madigan's daughter asking why grandma's crying only to have Madigan tell her to shut up and eat a Ding-Dong to Burstyn's determination to start pursuing her own dreams after Hackman leaves her, which means getting a beauty makeover and promptly taking herself to the nearest male strip show. These people are so endearing, even in their stupidity, that you want to send them postcards after the movie's over urging them to keep in touch.

> —*Michael Musto,* Saturday Review, *November/December 1985, 88.*

> The movie could be every errant husband's self-justifying fantasy. . . . He's a vigorous fifty-year-old, and the woman he falls for (a widow) is as fine and wise and loving as he is. The dishwater-dull wife wears an apron and watches game shows; her expressions of love for her husband are of the pathetic, lip-gnawing variety. So he has to be strong enough for the two of them when he leaves. The film goes on demeaning her. She keeps saying, "I didn't deserve this," as if she thought that life works in terms of whether you deserve things. And when she wins at bingo she carries on like a ninny. A series of scenes record her bitterness, her moping, and then her gradual awakening, which is possibly even more offensive. The sign- posts on her road to mental health include getting her hair dyed and going to a male-strip disco. At the end, she's preparing to "take some classes." (The husband doesn't need reeducation.)

> —*Pauline Kael,* The New Yorker, *2 December 1985, pp. 118, 121.*
> *Reprinted by permission. Copyright © by Pauline Kael. Originally in* The New Yorker.

3. Write a paragraph giving your opinion of the movie or show you described in exercise 1. Take a cue from the reviews that you have read in this chapter, and make your opinions as specific and pointed as you can.

CHAPTER SUMMARY

In this chapter you've studied

- summarizing other people's opinions
- smoothing out another writer's prose
- using tense consistently
- using semicolons and colons
- describing the plot of a movie or TV show
- expressing judgments

9

"Disporting in the Fountain": Deciding About Tone

Tone—one of those words that's easier to understand than to define—means the attitude of the writer toward what is being written. Tone depends upon the writer's intended *audience*, the *subject* being written about, and the *purpose* for doing the writing—all of which affect the choice of words.

SERIOUS TONE

Let us show you what we mean by providing some examples. The following paragraph addresses an *audience* of educated people. Notice that the *subject* (baseball) could easily have been presented in a light tone, but the *purpose* (to explain the ancient rituals that can be detected in the game) requires a more serious tone.

VOCABULARY

basilica	an early Christian church building
mosque	a moslem place of worship

mandala   a design symbolic of the universe in Oriental art
stupa   a dome-shaped Buddhist shrine

> Baseball diamonds organize space in much the same way as the basilica of St. Peter at Rome, the altar of heaven at Peking, and the great mosque at Mecca. What happens on a baseball diamond may seem to be only a sport, but the pattern of the field and the rules of the game also form a ritual.
>
> To look at a baseball diamond, as millions of Americans do for billions of hours every summer, is to contemplate a mandala: a design that aids meditation by drawing attention from its borders to its center. Within every baseball diamond is a mound of earth, a circle marking the center of a square, to which the focus of the game returns with every pitch. Like the burial mounds of native Americans, the stupas of Theravadin Buddhists, and the earth altars of Hindus, the pitcher's mound is an especially sacred space.

> —*Peter Gardella, "The Tao of Baseball,"* Harper's, *May 1986, p. 28.*

Notice these characteristics of word choice in the preceding passage: it has no contractions, no slang, no addressing of the reader as *you*, and no author evident (as would be the case if the writer used the first person, *I/my* or *we/our*). Notice also that the words chosen tend to be those used by educated people—not those of common, everyday speech. He chooses *organize* instead of *use* and *contemplate* instead of *think*, and he includes several difficult words related to the subject, such as *basilica, mosque, mandala, stupas.* This combination of a serious or neutral tone and the word choice just described produces what is called *formal English.* You should probably use formal English when you write anything serious—like academic papers, especially those involving research.

LIGHT TONE

The next paragraph illustrates a light tone, because the writer's purpose is to entertain a wide audience (the readers of *Newsweek* magazine) by making fun of a subject suitable for laughter—the trendy new look in luxury hotels.

Is it just my imagination or is something approaching clinical insanity now evident in the design and furnishing of American hotels? "There's a small hotel/By a wishing well/I wish that we were there together...." You remember the old song. You probably remember too those wonderful photos of Scott and Zelda dressed to the nines and disporting themselves in the fountain outside the Plaza in New York. Maybe you've even been to a grand hotel that looks out on Lake Como or Victoria Falls. Hotels, after all, have always been romantically associated with water. My question is this: who decided to bring the lake into the lobby?

—*Meg Greenfield, "Who Put the Lake in the Lobby?"* Newsweek, *13 January 1986, p. 76. Copyright 1986, by Newsweek, Inc. All Rights Reserved. Reprinted by Permission.*

Notice these characteristics of the word choice: the writer speaks in the first person (*my*), includes contractions (*there's*), uses some slang ("dressed to the nines"), and addresses the reader as *you*. In general, the words are easier to understand than those in the serious passage we presented first (except for the humorous, old-fashioned phrase, "disporting themselves in the fountain"). These kinds of word choices combine to produce what is called *informal English*, which can be written with any tone you find suitable for the subject and the audience. Most of the writing you will do following graduation will probably be in informal English (although not necessarily humorous, like the passage you just read.)

It's not, of course, a matter of just using the tone you *like* better. You need to know how to assume various tones suitable for both formal and informal writing as your audience and purpose demand.

KEY ESSAY

Rewrite the serious paragraph about ritual in baseball in a lighter tone using informal language. Your audience might be the readers of a college humor magazine or of a college newspaper.

Then rewrite the humorous paragraph about hotel decor in a serious tone using formal language. Your audience might be the readers of a magazine devoted to architecture or to hotel management.

Here's a reminder to help you decide what you need to change:

SERIOUS/FORMAL ENGLISH	LIGHTER/INFORMAL ENGLISH
No contractions	Contractions expected
No slang	Often some slang
No addressing reader as *you*	Reader addressed as *you*
No *I/me, we/our* (usually)	*I/me, we/our* expected
Complex vocabulary	Simple vocabulary

QUESTIONS FOR ANALYZING WRITING

Trade papers with another student. About that person's first paragraph (on rituals in baseball), answer these questions on a separate sheet:

1. Does the writer address the reader as *you*?
2. Does the writer use contractions?
3. Does the writer use slang? Is the slang appropriate?
4. Does the writer use simple, familiar language?
5. What audience (reader or readers) do you think this paragraph is written for? Is this audience different from the intended readers of the original, in your opinion?
6. Do you think the informal tone is suitable for the subject and the purpose, or was the paragraph more effective as originally written? Tell why or why not.

Now, about the second paragraph (on hotel decor), answer these questions on a separate sheet:

1. Does the writer avoid addressing the reader as *you*?
2. Does the writer avoid contractions?
3. Does the writer avoid slang?
4. Does the writer use complex language (fairly difficult words)?
5. What audience do you suppose this paragraph is now written for? What was the audience of the original?
6. Do you find the serious tone and formal language as effective for this material as the original light tone and informal language? Tell why or why not.

EXERCISES

SET A: WRITING FLUENTLY

1. Although you may never be required to write strictly to entertain your readers, you might want to try doing it just for fun. One means of achieving humor in writing involves reproducing dialect—that is, putting on paper the kind of language that people ordinarily use only in speech (called *colloquial language*). Dialects vary according to where the people using them live and who these people associate with. You've probably heard Eddie Murphy speak in black dialect to achieve humor. Here's an example in which Texan Larry L. King explains in his native dialect that Texas "macho" is only a myth:

TEXAS MACHO? TEXAS BEAUTIES? NOBLE ALAMO MARTYRS? THEY'RE ALL MYTHS, PARDNER!; A NATIVE SON DEBUNKS THE 10 BIGGEST MYTHS ABOUT THE LONE STAR STATE

Oh, yeah, you can still find a few honkey-tonks where somebody may break your jaw just because they need the practice. Gilley's in Pasadena and Billy Bob's in Fort Worth continue to challenge urban cowboys to test their bucking bulls, mechanical or real. Sweetwater still holds the annual Rattlesnake Roundup, where contestants pay $10 each to catch live poisonous critters and tote their biggest, meanest captives to the judge's stand in gunnysacks. (The winners get to eat all the fried snake they want and a future almost guaranteed to be free of folks messin' with them.) But all that used to be commonplace and now it's considered downright eccentric. Long time ago they quit letting you fight duels without the courts meddlin' in it, and if some dude's caught trifling with your Honey, you can't blow him away, invoke the Unwritten Law and go on about your bidness. The law's got as picky about that as they are about dadgummed jaywalking.

—TV Guide, *14 December 1985, p. 28 Reprinted with permission from* TV GUIDE® *Magazine and the author. Copyright © 1985 by Triangle Publications, Inc. Radnor, Pennsylvania.*

Even though King never uses the pronoun *I* in this paragraph, you can almost hear his voice. He uses contractions, slang, and even spelling to make the writing sound like west Texas speech (*bidness* for *business, meddlin'* for *meddling*). Notice that he not only addresses the reader as *you* (first sentence) but also uses the *impersonal you* ("Long time ago they quit letting you fight duels . . ."), with *you* meaning *anyone*. This use of *you* is frowned on in almost all writing except for humorous pieces, like King's, or in exactly reproduced conversations.

Now write a paragraph similar to King's (on any subject you want to ridicule) in which you reproduce as closely as you can a dialect that you know well. Try to make your spelling suggest the sound of the words. If you need another example, take a look at Mark Twain's *Adventures of Huckleberry Finn*.

2. Write a brief letter to the director of your student union, or student center, asking that "No Smoking" areas be designated in the main cafeteria and in the coffee shop. Adopt a serious tone and use formal language.

Now rewrite the same letter using a lighter tone and informal language addressed to the "Letters to the Editor" column of your school paper.

What changes did you make?

3. Identify the tone of the following paragraphs. Then try to decide why each writer chose that tone, and discuss how well suited it is for the intended audience. Determine whether the language used is mainly formal, informal, or colloquial English. In writing, explain what word choices in the passage helped you to decide.

> While no sane person would suggest that discrimination against smokers rises to the moral obscenity of discrimination based on race, sex, or religion, the trend is still pernicious. One might have hoped that one of the lessons we learned in the struggle to outlaw job discrimination is that the use of non-job-related criteria to control the distribution of jobs is perverse, counter productive, and dumb.
>
> —Bernar —Bernard Dushman, "A Burning Issue on the Job and Off" Newsweek, *13 January 1986, p. 9*.

> Tanks are heavy machinery at its heaviest and simplest in a time when respectable weapons abound in microcircuitry, frequency-agile radar, focal-plane arrays, and near-sentient

electronics. Modern tanks have many of these gewgaws and sometimes use them well, but they are essentially an incrustation of glitter. Remove the accretion of advanced whatnots, and the tank is still a hard object with a large gun. No matter how silly tanks may seem, no matter how archaic and unreliable, when one heaves out of the smoke and comes at you, you have a problem.

—*Fred Reed, "Tanked: Test-Driving the Army's M1,"*
Harper's, *February 1986, p. 64.*

There were three popular ways of stopping a bike—"coaster brake," "hand brake," and "hitting something." Less popular methods included accidentally sticking your foot in the front wheel or clamping hard on just the front hand brake, which made you do a tight little somersault over the handlebars.

Another sloppy way to stop was to get your pantcuff caught between the front sprocket and the chain, causing a sudden shift of weight to starboard. You slowly fell off the bike and scraped along the ground. The bike, still attached to your leg, jarred around on top of you until an axle bolt stuck in your ear.

—*Dereck Williamson, "The Mudbacks,"* Saturday Review,
June 1971, p. 6.

SET B: WRITING ACCURATELY

1. If you write unintentional sentence fragments, you should take care to correct them when you revise. Most readers remain seriously prejudiced against fragments—especially if those fragments appear for no apparent reason.

If you write fragments because you're careless about punctuation, at least your problem isn't difficult to correct. All you have to do is take more care in proofreading. But if you write fragments because you can't tell the difference between a complete sentence and a fragment, you have a problem.

First, you need to learn to distinguish between dependent and independent clauses,* because if you put a period after a dependent clause, you've caused a fragment:

• *Fragment*: Because Henry married before his graduation.

---

* A clause is a group of words having a subject and a verb. Independent clauses can stand alone as sentences; dependent clauses can't.

It's the subordinating word *because* that creates the problem. It makes the clause depend on another one to complete its meaning.

● *Complete*: Henry married before his graduation.

This is an independent clause because it doesn't leave you hanging. If you want to keep the subordinating word, you can simply attach the dependent clause to an independent clause and have a complete sentence:

● *Complete*: Because Henry married before his graduation, his father cut off his allowance.

Here are the subordinating words that you need to be wary of:

after	only	unless
although, though	since	until, till
as, as if	so as	when, whenever
because	so far as	where, wherever
before	so that	which, whichever
if, even if	that	while
in order that	who, whoever	whose
whether		

Whenever you begin a statement with one of these words, be sure to attach it to another clause so that the whole sounds complete. Notice the difference between these examples:

● *Not a sentence*: Although she is a good athlete otherwise.
● *Now a sentence*: She is a good athlete otherwise.
● *Now a sentence*: Although she is a good athlete otherwise, Selma sometimes swears at the umpire.

● *Not a sentence*: Unless she sees the error of her ways.
● *Now a sentence*: She sees the error of her ways.
● *Now a sentence*: Unless she sees the error of her ways, Selma may get tossed off the team.

Now, rewrite the following paragraph and eliminate any sentence fragments.

Fall and spring are the best times to picnic in the Midwest. Which is where we live. As soon as spring comes and the snow melts and the rain stops. We want to go out to Moraine View State Park and eat by the lake. Although the wind is usually blowing too hard there to keep the food on a picnic table. Last fall we had just found a perfect spot and spread the lunch out. When a gust of wind picked up our plates like Frisbees and sailed them straight into the water. We gave up our lake view then. After repacking all of the food in our picnic basket and our drinks in our Styrofoam cooler. With much grumbling, we hiked back into the forest to a spot out of the wind. Where we once more unpacked our feast and spread it out to eat. This time we got the sandwiches and potato salad out onto plates. Which the ants immediately found also. Seymour kept saying they don't eat much. But that isn't the point. Who wants to share a scrumptious potato salad with a bunch of ants? Maybe no time is a good time to picnic in the Midwest.

2. You also can end up with a fragment in several other ways. For instance, some words are treacherous because they sound like verbs but aren't. Some words ending in -*ing* suggest action (going, tapping, baking, romping) but aren't complete verbs unless they have a helping verb with them (am going, was tapping, are baking, have been romping, etc.). So, if you've written only a *phrase* (a group of words without a subject and a verb), you may need to attach it to the sentence before or after it. Or, you could change the -*ing* word into a complete verb.

Notice the differences in the following examples:

- *Not a sentence*:   Romping with my new friend.
- *Now a sentence*:   Romping with my new friend exhausted me.
- *Now a sentence*:   I *have been romping* with my new friend.

You need to be careful, also, not to leave part of a sentence dangling by itself, like this:

- Fat Clyde just lies there. Like a huge meatloaf.

Just attach the phrase to the preceding sentence. Use a dash if you want emphasis; use no punctuation if you don't:

- Fat Clyde just lies there—like a huge meatloaf.
- Fat Clyde just lies there like a huge meatloaf.

Rewrite the following paragraph to eliminate any fragments. Use dashes sparingly—only if you want emphasis.

> Fasting is one way to lose weight. But not necessarily a good one. Especially if you tend to be sick a lot. You need the vitamins and minerals that food provides. In order to stay healthy. Slimming down twenty pounds in a week may seem like a triumph. Unless you can't stop. And go on losing twenty pounds even after you're skinny. Then, if you find you can't eat, or if you do manage to eat and the food won't stay down. You could be in big trouble. Trouble so bad that even doctors couldn't help you. Like Karen Carpenter with anorexia. You would be wiser to lose weight more slowly. And more safely.

3. Less frequent than fragments but even more bothersome to readers are sentences that run together without any punctuation at all between them, like this:

● Aardvarks are not very bright turtles are even dumber.

Such disasters, called *fused sentences* (or *run-ons*), may result simply from sheer, unpardonable carelessness, or they may result because the writer fails to recognize where one sentence ends and another begins. If you know you have a problem with run-ons, you need to check every sentence as you proofread to be sure that you haven't run some of them together. You can correct the problem in several ways:

● Aardvarks aren't very bright; turtles are even dumber.
● Aardvarks aren't very bright, but turtles are even dumber.
● Although aardvarks aren't very bright, turtles are even dumber.

For practice, rewrite the following paragraph to eliminate any run-on sentences.

> A word processor can save you time it can make revising easier. Anytime you write something that someone else is going to read you should polish your prose. Sometimes you'll need to go through several drafts you can accomplish this revision without retyping the whole piece if you're using a word processor. You can change words you can move sentences or whole paragraphs around. You can add sentences or take out sentences. Even an incompetent typist can produce perfect copy the machine allows you to correct typos without a trace.

SET C: WRITING LOGICALLY AND COHERENTLY

1. Think of three audiences (intended readers) for whom you might write a paragraph telling how to overcome a specific bad habit (like smoking, drinking, taking drugs, procrastinating, or being late for work). Try to think of groups who would be widely different in ages and attitudes. For instance, you might offer instruction to a group of police officers, a group of teenaged gang members, and a group of high school teachers. After you choose three groups, write out a list of the characteristics of each audience: what would be their approximate ages and their general attitudes toward manners, religion, morality, discipline, entertainment, education, and money?

When you have recorded all the pertinent information you can think of about each prospective audience, trade papers with a classmate. Then, help each other try to think of any other traits that might be useful to consider.

Finally, decide, in consultation with your partner, what tone and language level (formal, informal, or colloquial) would be appropriate to use in writing for each audience.

2. Select one of the groups that you described in the preceding exercise, and write a paragraph telling those people how to overcome a bad habit. Be sure to adopt the tone and language level you decided would be appropriate for that audience.

3. Go through the papers you have written for this course as well as any you have written for other classes. Decide what tone and language level you adopted for each, and explain in writing why your choices were good or poor.

CHAPTER SUMMARY

In this chapter you have studied

- using a serious tone
- using formal English
- using a light tone
- using informal English
- using a humorous tone
- using colloquial English
- avoiding sentence fragments
- avoiding fused sentences (or run-ons)
- analyzing potential audiences

10

SUDDEN HOOD FLY-UP: REVISING FOR CLARITY

The following is part of an actual recall letter that a car manufacturer sent to owners of possibly defective automobiles. Imagine that you received the letter; read it through and try to figure out what's wrong with your car. (We have numbered the lines so that you can more easily discuss the letter after you have read it.)

1	A defect which involves the possible failure of a frame sup-
2	port plate may exist on your vehicle. This plate (front suspen-
3	sion pivot bar support plate) connects a portion of the front
4	suspension to the vehicle frame, and its failure could affect
5	vehicle directional control, particularly during heavy brake
6	application. In addition, your vehicle may require adjustment
7	service to the hood secondary catch system. The secondary
8	catch may be misaligned so that the hood may not be
9	adequately restrained to prevent hood fly-up in the event the
10	primary catch is inadvertently left unengaged. Sudden hood
11	fly-up beyond the secondary catch while driving could impair
12	driver visibility. In certain circumstances, occurrence of either
13	of the above conditions could result in vehicle crash without
14	prior warning.

Can you figure out what the problem is? Would you take your car in for service?

In 1983 the General Accounting Office (GAO), the auditing arm of Congress, made a report on automobile recalls. The report said that public recall notices are difficult to understand and contribute to poor consumer participation in recall programs —only 50 percent take their cars back for adjustment. The GAO paid a linguist $23,000 to write an understandable form letter. How would you like to learn to make $23,000?

KEY ESSAY

Your task is to rewrite the recall letter and make it clear. We will take you through the first two sentences, and you can then finish the revision on your own (with just a few pointers from us). Reread the recall notice, as best you can, and then consider these criticisms of its style:

1. There are almost no people in this letter. Cars are actually made, driven, and fixed by people. Yet this recall notice contains only three words that refer to a person: *your*, used twice, and *driver.* There are no other personal pronouns—like *I, me, we, they, he, she, her*—and no other nouns that refer to human beings. This is one reason the letter does not communicate—it isn't written with humans in mind.
2. Another problem with the writing is that many important actions are not directly expressed. For instance, the noun *failure* (in lines 1 and 5) suggests an action, but the verb *fail* is not used. The same is true for the phrases "vehicle directional control" and "brake application" (lines 5–7). What do these words mean? Well, a very simple way to restate those implied actions is "You won't be able to steer your car when you apply the brakes."
3. A further difficulty is the use of too many words: unnecessary words ("a portion of the front suspension"), undefined terms ("frame support plate"), and complicated words ("vehicle," "adequately restrained," and "inadvertently left unengaged").

DOING A REWRITE

Having spotted these problems, let's rewrite the first sentence. Move the person to the front of the sentence, take out the meaningless terminology, change "may exist" to *may have*, and you will come up with this simple statement: *Your car may have a defective part.*

The second sentence is a compound sentence. Change "this plate" to *it*, and cut out a lot of unneeded words: *It connects the front suspension to the frame.* Next, revise the indirect actions into simple verbs and use *you* as the personal subject of these actions: *If it fails, you won't be able to steer, especially if you brake hard.*

All right, now it's your turn. First compare what we did to the first two sentences with the original version of the letter. Then write our revised sentences on a piece of paper, and continue to revise the recall notice. Make every sentence clear and direct. Two hints: (1) you will probably need to use the pronoun *we* for the people who make and fix the car; and (2) you will find other actions implied by "adjustment service" (*adjust*), "fly-up" (*fly up*), "driving" (*drive*), "visibility" (*see*), "occurrence" (*occur*), and "warning" (*warn*).

ANALYZING REVISION

Exchange your revision with someone else in class. Read your partner's rewrite and then, on a separate sheet of paper, put these headings (one near the top, one halfway down):

1. Sentences that are better than my revisions
2. Sentences that could be improved with more revision

Put at least one sentence from your partner's revised letter under each heading. Return this sheet with the rewrite. When you get your own letter back, work on the sentence(s) that your partner said could be improved.

EXERCISES

SET A: WRITING FLUENTLY

1. In the original recall letter the phrases "adjustment service" and "brake application" are examples of putting important actions into noun form. In these phrases *adjust* was expressed as "adjust-ment" and *apply* was expressed as "application." Here are some

more examples:

ACTION	NOUN
discover	discovery
compete	competition
resist	resistance
improve	improvement

We change verbs to nouns frequently in English, and a writer can take advantage of this flexibility of the language to express an abstract thought in a clear way. But often making this change hides an important action and results in wordiness:

- The FBI conducted an *investigation* into the crime.
- The administration has no *expectation* that it will achieve a deficit *reduction*.

Both of these sentences would be shorter and clearer if the italicized nouns were expressed as simple actions:

- The FBI *investigated* the crime.
- The administration does not *expect* to *reduce* the deficit.

Rewrite the following sentences by changing the italicized nouns into simple verbs. Take out or change other words to simplify the style and clarify the ideas.

Example: Our *discussion* of the rules lasted for a long time.
Revision: We *discussed* the rules a long time.

a. They have a *need* for *reanalysis* of the case.
b. Their *presentation* of the data was not confused.
c. The teacher conducted an *examination* of his student's knowledge.
d. Our *feeling* is that your *decision* on the issue is necessary.
e. The board will make *inquiry* regarding the problem of *overcrowdedness* in the rooms of the dormitory.
f. Continued *driving* with a failed bearing could result in *disengagement* of the axle shaft and adversely affect vehicle *control*.

   2. In addition to expressing important actions in simple verbs (rather than in nouns), you also want the *agent* of an important

action to be the subject of the verb. An agent is the person or thing responsible for the main action in a sentence:

(agent)   (action)
● The   FBI   investigated   the   crime.

Sometimes the agent appears some place other than the subject:

● *Determination* of policy occurs in the *mayor's* office.

When you take the important action out of a noun (*determination*), you can also make the agent (*mayor*) the subject of the sentence:

(agent)   (action)
● The   mayor   determines   policy.

Here are some more examples, with the agents and actions in italics:

Example: *Attempts* were made by the *police department* to find the lost child.
Revision: The *police department attempted* to find the lost child.
Example: The *appearance* of the *defendant* in court was on May 10.
Revision: The *defendant appeared* in court on May 10.

Sometimes a sentence contains no agent for its main action:

● There should be no *hesitation* in saying no.

You would have to invent an agent if you wanted to rewrite this sentence:

● *You* should not *hesitate* to say no.
● A *person* should not *hesitate* to say no.

The context will help you come up with an agent when you revise a weak sentence.

   Rewrite the following sentences in a more direct way. Use the agents of the actions as subjects. Both agents and nouns made from verbs have been italicized for you.

a. A *promise* to cut taxes was made to the American people by the *President*.

b. *Agreement* on the terms of the contract came from *both sides*.

c. There is *competition* among the *three brothers* for their father's approval.

d. *Sending* of the parts has been carried out by the *shipping department*.

e. Accomplishment of the gradual land *clearing* was achieved by the *Park Service*.

In rewriting the following sentences you will have to invent agents:

f. A *solution* to the problem of teenage suicide may never be found.

g. There was no *suspicion* of a scandal in the White House.

3. Most likely, you have a machine or product that doesn't work right. Write a clear paragraph that tells exactly what's not right about the thing, so someone who is thinking about getting the same thing will know what to expect.

SET B: WRITING ACCURATELY

1. Make the following sentences more streamlined and effective by removing colorless, unnecessary, and uninformative words. You may have to jot down several versions before you come up with a clear, concise sentence. Here are some ways to improve the economy of these sentences:

Remove Redundancy—eliminate the repetition of words or phrases similar in meaning:

Redundant: As a rule freshmen do not usually cut class.
Improved: As a rule freshmen do not cut class.

Redundant: Sheila's costume was round in shape and blue in color.
Improved: Sheila's costume was round and blue.

Avoid Padding—eliminate vague and general words and phrases like *element, factor, aspect*, and *in terms of*:

Padded: The important factor to remember in a teaching situation is the attention span aspect.

Streamlined: We should remember attention span when teaching.

Padded: Constant lateness is a quality that your friends find insulting.

Streamlined: Your friends find your constant lateness insulting.

Cut Out Deadwood—eliminate expressions like *who was* or *which is* when they are not useful:

Deadwood: The shirt which is torn is my uncle's.
Streamlined: The torn shirt is my uncle's.

Deadwood: The woman who was chair of the committee cut the discussion short.
Streamlined: The chair of the committee stopped the discussion.

Eliminate Pretentious Words—substitute clear, understandable language for inflated wordiness:

Pretentious: I can say with sincere veracity that my desire to scale the heights of success is most genuine.
Direct: I truly want to succeed.

Refer to the preceding suggestions when revising these sentences:

a. The point of her talk was to explain how people can reduce excess salt from their diets of ordinary food.
b. The fact is that stories which appear in newspapers are old news by the time readers get their papers because television can be right on the scene as the story breaks.
c. The man who was wearing a green shirt made every attempt possible to rescue the dog which was small and brown as it teetered precariously on a log in the river which was raging.
d. The different areas of occupation have fascinated me since I was but a student in high school, and I am still carefully cogitating about what course my future program of study will pursue.
e. In all estimates of the difficulties at hand, Carrie Stone has maintained an air of complete control and calm which is certainly admirable, to say the least. *We admire the complete*
f. There seems to be from time to time the feeling that there could be more efficiency in assembling our products which are produced on our assembly line. *we feel*

2. Revise and combine the following sets of sentences so that they will be clear and readable. You may have to correct any shifts—from one person to another, from singular to plural, from past to present—that interfere with a reader's understanding of the sentences. Here is an example:

Unclear: Many mistakes are made by new operators. The experienced operator could make just as many if they were not careful.

Clear: New operators make many mistakes, but experienced operators can make just as many if they are not careful.

a. Elmo was wearing his best suit for the party. He feels sick. Nan meets him at the door. She is dressed in jeans and a shirt.
b. The dance tape is terrific. It was produced by an old tape producer Bill Sherman. He sure knew what he was doing when he did that.
c. It's a good thing for a person to be an excellent swimmer if they're going sailing. You never know when a storm might come up suddenly and capsize your boat.
d. Del Martin and I planned the block party. You never realize the amount of work involved. You become involved in a project like that.
e. The Indian in New England has made some surprising discoveries in the past year. They realize that treaties are still on the books which said they still have ownership of much land.

3. Review your last three essays for this class. Pick out two paragraphs from any of these essays to revise: cut out deadwood, streamline the style, and combine sentences for greater smoothness.

SET C: WRITING LOGICALLY AND COHERENTLY

1. Combine and revise the following sentences into a clear, coherent paragraph. (*Coherent* means that the sentences hold together and flow smoothly from one to the next.)

• Patrice accidentally locked all her keys in the house.
• She was leaving for school.
• She could not get back into the house.

- She could not drive the car.
- She felt like throwing in the towel.
- She felt like going fishing.
- She could not get her fishing gear out of the garage.
- The garage was locked too.

Try to combine these eight sentences into a paragraph that contains only three or four sentences.

2. Rewrite the paragraph that you just constructed. Add more details to the story, and expand it to twice its length. Bring the story to a clear and definite close.

3. Look at your last three essays in this class. Choose one that contains some paragraphs that need to be revised and expanded. Rewrite these paragraphs, improving the style and adding more information and details to the content.

CHAPTER SUMMARY

In this chapter you've studied

- rewriting unclear prose
- using active verbs
- expressing ideas forcefully
- cutting out unnecessary words
- making paragraphs coherent
- adding details

11

"THANKS FOR NOT SMOKING": SIMPLE PROBLEM SOLVING

People write to "Dear Abby" because they need help in solving personal or social problems. One recent issue that Abby and her readers have been wrestling with involves the conflict between smokers and nonsmokers. As Abby points out, many nonsmokers are too timid or too polite to speak up and confront those who pollute their breathing space. Here is a typical letter.

Dear Abby:

I am a schoolteacher with a serious bronchial condition. The doctor told me I should put a sign up in my apartment reading "Thanks for not smoking."

Everyone who has come to visit me has respected that request, and I really appreciated it. Last week I had a few guests who had never visited me before. When one of them saw the sign, she said: "Don't think I am staying here and not smoking. Give me an ashtray!"

When I told her I didn't have any ashtrays she asked for a dish. I refused. I served coffee, and she and the others smoked and used their cups for ashtrays.

Abby, I couldn't believe it. I didn't want to hurt them, but I hurt myself. That night I couldn't sleep, and the next day I couldn't use my voice to speak to my students.

Please print this. I know they read your column. It might help. Sign this . . .

Off My Chest

—From The Best of Dear Abby *(New York: Andrews and McNeel, 1981), pp. 101–102.*

KEY ESSAY

Write a letter to "Dear Abby" in which you offer advice to "Off My Chest." How can she convince people not to smoke in her presence without losing her friends? Consider the problem thoughtfully and offer your best solution.

PROBLEM SOLVING AS INVENTION

Knowing some problem-solving techniques will help you even more than "Dear Abby"—in your daily life, as well as in your writing. The basic approach involves breaking the problem down into smaller pieces. If, for instance, you were trying to decide whether to get married or not, you would need to think of all the changes—major and minor—that marriage would make in your life. You would do the same thing if you were going to write something about the general topic of "Should a person marry while still in college?" First, you brainstorm for ideas by asking yourself what changes are likely to occur, jotting down whatever comes to mind. The major changes that you think of could eventually become the main headings in your outline; the minor changes could be grouped under those major headings as supporting details.

Probably you'd want to carry the problem solving at least one step further and evaluate the changes. Would they be positive or negative? Here you need to list everything you consider positive on one sheet of paper and everything you consider negative on another. Then, weigh the evidence in your mind. It's not necessarily just a matter of looking to see which list is longer, because one list may contain a large number of minor items, whereas the other list may contain a small number of crucial changes.

Whenever you write anything—a letter, a memo, a report, an essay—that involves persuading others to agree with your point of view, you should consider using problem-solving techniques. You will find that systematic thinking helps you intelligently sort out your ideas and draw conclusions about those ideas.

QUESTIONS FOR ANALYZING WRITING

Read a classmate's letter to "Dear Abby" offering advice to "Off My Chest." Then, on a separate sheet, respond in writing to the following questions:

1. Is there any evidence to indicate that the writer engaged in problem solving before writing? That is, are there thoughtful suggestions or observations that sound as if they might have resulted from this prewriting activity?
2. Do you agree with the writer's advice? Mention points that you find effective. Also note specific points that you consider wrong or illogical, and explain your views.
3. Do you think the letter is persuasive? Does the writer at least make you consider a new viewpoint? If so, what are the most convincing points? If not, can you explain what the writer needs to do in order to make a better case?
4. Do you think that "Off My Chest" would consider this a good solution to the problem? Explain why or why not.
5. Do you think "Dear Abby" would print this letter? If so, why? If not, try to suggest revisions that would make it acceptable.

When you get back the first draft of your own letter, revise it using any of your classmate's suggestions that seem helpful.

EXERCISES

SET A: WRITING FLUENTLY

1. Write a letter to a close friend attending another university advising this person against getting married before graduation. Or, take the opposite approach and try to convince your friend that

getting married while still in college is a good plan. Be sure to go through the problem-solving activities suggested in the previous section before you write. You may want to discuss both advantages and disadvantages as you make a case for or against the marriage. Remember that in order to be convincing, you must offer specific examples.

2. The following letter to "Dear Abby" argues in favor of allowing people to smoke if they feel like it:

> Dear Abby:
> I resent the way people are now trying to make smokers feel like second-class citizens.
> Smoking is a nervous habit, right? Well, I put up with the nervous habits of others. Some folks crack their knuckles, others clear their throats, some have nervous coughs, or they sniff. People with nervous tics also make me nervous, but I don't mention it.
> So, since smoking is also a nervous habit, why can't people be as tolerant of *my* nervous habit as I am of theirs?
>
> Pipe Smoker
>
> —*From* The Best of Dear Abby *(New York: Andrews and McNeel, 1981), p. 104.*

Analyze the logic of this letter and write a response to "Pipe Smoker."

3. Think of a problem in your life that's bothering you—lack of money, lack of friends, too many friends, too much work, too little time. Make sure it is some problem that you genuinely need to solve. Work through the problem-solving techniques mentioned earlier. Then write a report or a letter to yourself suggesting at least two reasonable ways to improve your situation.

Week 8

SET B: WRITING ACCURATELY   *Word Confusion*

1. In our language we have a number of look-alike or sound-alike words that confuse writers no end. You know the trouble-makers: words like *its/it's*, *effect/affect*, *to/too/two*, and *there/their/they're*. If you choose the wrong one of these pesky terms, you may upset a reader who knows the difference. You may know the

difference but use the wrong one out of carelessness. But, if you—like lots of other people—really don't know which one to choose, you need to consult the following list as you tidy up the final draft of everything you write.

Accept   I accept your offer. [means *to receive* or *take* or *agree with*]
Except   They took everything except my hamster. [means *but*] We will except Oprah from the rule. [means to *exclude*]

Affect   The cold weather affects my sinuses. [means *influences*]
Effect   The cold weather has a bad effect on my sinuses. [means the *result* of being affected]

Its   Your idea has much in its favor. [possessive of *it*; like the other possessive pronouns—*his, hers, ours, theirs*, and so on—this word does NOT need an apostrophe]
It's   It's too late to change your mind. [contraction of *it is*; like all the other contractions—*can't, won't, isn't, don't*, and so on—this word DOES use an apostrophe]

Lie   Joe lies around the house like a rug. [means *to recline*]
He lay down last night after dinner. [past tense]
He has lain down every evening. [past participle]

Lay   Where did I lay my pen down just now? [means *to put*; present tense]
I laid it on the table yesterday. [past tense]
Where have I laid that pesky pen? [past participle]

Loose   Sam has a screw loose. [means *undone* or *unchecked* or *not tight*]
Lose   Did you lose your head? [means *to misplace* or *part with accidentally*]

Quiet   Please be quiet; the cat's asleep. [means *silent*]
Quite   The kitty's quite tired from being out all night. [means *very*]

Rise   The sun also rises. [means *to go up*]
Raise   That noise will raise the dead. [means *to cause to go up*]

Sit   I like to sit by a window. [you know what that means]
Set   Please set my coffee beside me. [means *to place*]

Than   Carlos dances better than I do. [used in comparisons]
Then   He screamed; then he fainted. [means *next*]

Their   It wasn't their fault. [the possessive pronoun, hence no
          apostrophe]
They're They're sure to be late. [contraction of *they are*]
There   Did you look over there? [indicates a place]

To   Try to say something nice to Henry. [used with action words
         and with nouns]
Too   Speak to Hortense, too. [means *also*]
         She is too timid to argue. [means excessively]
Two   Those two are just alike. [means the number]

Weather   The weather was humid this winter. [means climate]
Whether   Can you tell whether it will rain or not? [suggests an
            alternative or choice]

Whose   Whose llama is this? [possessive pronoun, hence no apos-
          trophe]
Who's   Who's coming to dinner? [contraction of *who is*]

Your   Is that your llama? [possessive pronoun, hence no apos-
          trophe]
You're You're not allowed to have llamas here. [contraction of
          you are]

Another common difficulty occurs with words ending in *-ed*. Often we don't pronounce the *-ed* ending when talking (as in *used, supposed, prejudiced,* and *asked*). We say, "Henry is the most prejudice person I know," and nobody minds. But in writing, the *-ed* must be there. Remember to check those words in revising and make sure you've not left off an *-ed*.

Now, an exercise to let you see how well you cope with some of these words that cause difficulty. The following paragraph contains numerous errors in word choice. (We counted seventeen.) Rewrite each sentence, correcting any mistakes you find.

Thelma, as she lit yet another cigarette, ask Theodore if his body was use to the affects of nicotine yet. Theodore shook his head and said he suppose it gave him bad breath and adversely effected his lungs. "Its a dangerous habit, all right, smoking is," observed Thelma, sitting her matches down. "My main objection concerns it's tendency to stain my teeth," she added. Theodore admitted that he coughed a lot in the mornings. "Often I have a headache, to, which I'm sure comes from smoking," he complained. "Oh, I know," agreed Thelma, "and every so often I chose to quit, but its to hard!" "Let's lie down some rules for quitting and than stick too them," suggested Theodore. "I think that's a great idea!" declared Thelma, and they crushed out they're cigarettes in a salute two better health.

2. Write sentences of your own (as many as needed) in which you use each of the following words correctly. You may want help from your dictionary in order to complete this exercise.

its	then	there	affected
used	supposed	effect	lain
you're	it's	their	set
they're	lead	laid	raise
too	than	rise	quite
weather	your	whether	
principle	quiet	advise	
disinterested	advice	uninterested	

3. Dashes and parentheses are used for basically the same thing—to set off material from the rest of the sentence.* But notice this difference: use dashes if you want to call attention to the material being set off; use parentheses if you want to downplay (*not* call attention to) the material being set off. If you don't want to do either one, you can simply set off the material with commas. These choices are mainly a matter of style. Remember not to use dashes or parentheses too often; they will lose their effectiveness and merely clutter your prose.

- Clarence Konek—the absolute love of my life—just dumped me for another woman.
- Clarence Konek, my ex-boyfriend, is seeing someone else now.
- Clarence Konek (a former friend of mine) is engaged to Clarissa Cartwright.

---

* Note: You make a dash on your typewriter by striking two hyphens in a row with no space between the words and the hyphens.

Copy the following paragraph, substituting either dashes or parentheses for the commas—or else leaving the commas as they are—depending upon whether or not you want to emphasize the ideas set off in each sentence. Be prepared to explain why you made your choices.

> The Edwardian era, during the reign of Edward VII, was a period of opulent tastes and lavish entertaining. Some consider it a time of decadence, shockingly free in manners and morals. Several ladies in high social circles, several of the most beautiful ones, engaged His Majesty's amorous attentions. King Edward was thought by some to be a man of loose morals, a libertine even. But he was still admired and respected by all, or almost all, of his subjects.

SET C: WRITING LOGICALLY AND COHERENTLY

1. The letter of request in Figure 11–1 is unlikely to bring the desired response. Revise it until you are sure that its tone is suitable and the request is clearly stated. Be sure also that you include the information necessary to permit the reader to answer the letter easily. You may first want to study the guidelines in Chapter 15 (Set C, Exercise 2) for writing a successful letter of request.

2. Write a letter to the registrar of your college pointing out what you perceive to be a problem with the registration procedures. Explain the problem clearly, giving examples of the inconvenience caused to students because of it. Then, suggest a solution. If your solution involves expense for the college (like hiring another student worker), point out that the cost is nominal and well worth it. Remember to extend thanks to the registrar in your concluding paragraph for his or her consideration of your ideas.

If your registration system happens to be perfect, write instead to the campus administrator in charge of some other area, like the cafeteria or the library or the parking regulations—or wherever you perceive a problem that you think you can solve.

3. Write a letter to your school newspaper arguing that college athletes should be paid salaries for performing in intercollegiate athletics (or that student musicians, debaters, or actors and actresses should receive salaries for performing). Or, argue the reverse: that college athletes (or musicians, debaters, actors and

```
                                      428 West Pine St.
                                      Hudson, IL  61748
                                      Jan. 7th




Music Corporation of America
247 Broadway
New York, New York 10021

Hi!
        I'm writing a paper for a class and I need some
information about your business.  The paper is going to be on
women in the music business, so could you send me some
material on that?
        I haven't got a thesis down yet, but I'm thinking it
might be fun to do something on the history of women
technicians or the history of women drummers or what ways
women musicians are different than men, or something like
that.  I'm just not sure.  Anyway, if you could send me
whatever you have on those subjects, then I could get started
on this darned paper.
        I hope you don't take too long, because the paper is due
two weeks from Friday.
        Thanks a bunch,

        Bob Smithers

Robert Smithers
```

Figure 11–1   Letter to Revise.

actresses) already receive too much compensation in tuition and fee waivers and free trips for doing something that should be done voluntarily as part of their educational experience.

Structure your letter so that you conclude with your strongest point. Because your audience reads your final paragraph last, you want to leave them with a good impression. And don't forget the need for specific details in order to be convincing.

CHAPTER SUMMARY

In this chapter you've studied

- using problem solving in writing
- choosing between words that are often confused
- adding *-ed* to *ask, suppose, prejudice,* and *use*
- using dashes and parentheses
- revising for tone and clarity
- writing letters to persuade

12

NO MORE SANTA CLAUS: DEALING WITH DISSONANCE

When you were a little kid you probably believed in Santa Claus or the Easter Bunny, or both. Somewhere along the line you found out that these cherished characters were fictional. The truth may have been a little painful, but that was part of growing up. Then you learned that the discoveries got more serious: teachers can be wrong, parents won't always bail you out, honesty may not be the best policy. These collisions with reality hurt, but they also teach us a lot about the world we live in. The following essay, written by a freshman at Illinois State University, will tell you how one young man learned some unexpected truths about racism.

VOCABULARY

dilemma	predicament, difficult choice
ethical	involving standards of right and wrong
pervasive	present everywhere
naivete	lack of perception or informed judgment
repugnant	offensive, distasteful

DISTINCTLY LACKING

I grew up in a multiracial neighborhood, Hyde Park, on the south side of Chicago. I say multiracial, but since I attended public schools my particular society was predominantly black. At my eighth-grade graduation I was one of only five whites in a class of three hundred. When I was fourteen, my family moved to Wilmette, an almost entirely white suburb north of Chicago. This move was quite a cultural shock and led to a most painful emotional and ethical dilemma, one that I have still not completely resolved.

Growing up as a white kid in Hyde Park was at times like leading a double life. At home I spoke and behaved like any other white, midwestern child. At school and in the streets, however, I spoke what I guess one would call the Black American dialect. It had its own vocabulary and sentence structure. For example, "I be scrapin' fo' the crib, an' shine on some D-ho's, man, I be fencin' it straight" meant, approximately, "If I was walking home and saw some gang members, I would cut through people's yards to get home." It was not just language, though, but a culture I partially absorbed. I listened strictly to black radio stations and was basically ignorant of most white rock and roll.

Finding myself, at fourteen, among people who listened to different music, who dressed and talked like squares, and who all seemed to have their own cars and money, was a shock. I felt adrift. I was a stranger and made no friends for quite a while. Loneliness finally compelled me to accept these kids as they were, and I made friends quickly. But I was so eager for company that I made a compromise that shames me to this day.

The white people of Hyde Park were, almost by definition, liberal in their attitudes toward blacks. Indeed, among some conservative Chicagoans, the term "Hyde Park Liberal" is quite a damning label. In this environment, I grew up thinking that white bigots were restricted to certain southwestern sections of Chicago and to states below the Mason-Dixon line.

The pervasive and casual racism of the upper-middle class whites of the northern suburbs shocked me out of my naivete. Many of these people called themselves liberal, but they were so only when black people remained far away. I remember the stares I received while walking along the Kenilworth beach with two of my black friends who had come to visit me. I also remember the Kenilworth police car that kept hovering around us.

What did I do, surrounded by an attitude and opinions which I found morally wrong and personally repugnant? The answer is that I did nothing. Under the usual high school pressures to make friends and be popular, I smiled and kept silent as these ignorant young people casually tossed out clichés and slurs about people they had almost no experience with. I comfort myself with the knowledge that I was young and lonely, but I still think about that time and wince with regret.

Things did get better. I did find some people whose attitudes were not so troublesome, and eventually my friends knew that I was "touchy" about some subjects, which were not brought up anymore in my presence. Today I rarely let an acquaintance use the word "nigger" without politely pointing out that I find the term distasteful. I cannot forget, though, that when it came down to a choice between having easy companionship and following the dictates of my closely held beliefs, I found myself distinctly lacking.

—Jason T. Hurst. Reprinted with permission.

KEY ESSAY

Think of a situation like Jason's—one which presented you with a moral or intellectual choice. Perhaps a good friend asked you to give her financial and moral support for getting an abortion, and you're opposed to abortion. Or maybe your parents got divorced, and you had to choose which one to live with. Perhaps a friend or relative you like a lot told you that he or she is gay, and you were taught that homosexuality is wrong. What did you do? How did you solve the dilemma? Did you have to compromise, as Jason did? Would you do the same thing again?

In this essay you will be writing about "dissonance," which can be defined as "harsh disagreement between strongly opposed or conflicting positions." Dissonance is a challenging subject, but you can depend on lots of reader interest—we all experience dissonance and we like to hear how other people deal with their problems. Isn't that what soap operas are all about? Don't turn your life into a soap opera—your readers will know right away if you're making your situation up—but be as honest as you can about how you wrestled with a painful incident in your life.

DEFINE THE CONFLICT

You should begin your essay by defining the conflict and giving your readers enough background about the situation to help them understand why you did whatever it is you did. Here is an example in which the writer took two paragraphs to set out her dilemma:

> Because we are human beings with free will, we often make mistakes. The consequences of those mistakes can be annoying, aggravating, painful, even deadly. My friend, Mary, made such a mistake that put me in a difficult situation. Mary got pregnant. Not by herself, of course, but it was her problem alone. She came to me for help, and I will never be sure if what I did was right or wrong.
>
> Mary asked me to loan her money for an abortion and to take her to her appointment. As a Catholic, I have always believed that abortion is murder and that it is wrong. I did not know what to do: help my friend by putting my own opinions to one side, or abandon a good person in trouble who had already been abandoned by the man she loved. Rather than making judgments and iron-fast decisions, I talked to Mary about her opinion of the whole situation.

Once you have given your audience the necessary background, you are ready to explain how you handled the dissonance and then to comment on how you feel about the experience now.

QUESTIONS FOR ANALYZING WRITING

As usual, exchange papers with a classmate, read his or her essay, and answer the following questions in writing.

1. Does the first sentence get your attention? Could it be improved? How would you revise it?

2. Do you understand how the dilemma arose? If not, what else do you need to know?
3. Can you follow the explanation of how the writer dealt with the problem? If not, which points seem unclear to you?
4. Do you know how the author now feels about the situation and its resolution? Do you think he or she is being completely honest? If not, what points seem incomplete or insincere?
5. What details struck you as convincing and authentic?

When you get your own paper back, study the answers to the questions and make any changes that will improve your essay before you hand it in to your teacher.

EXERCISES

SET A: WRITING FLUENTLY

1. In his essay entitled "On Being 17, Bright, and Unable to Read," David Raymond introduces the reader to the subject by re-counting a relevant incident. In other words, he uses a narrative opening. Read the opening, and then revise the beginning of your dissonance essay in imitation of Raymond's introduction.

> One day a substitute teacher picked me to read aloud from the textbook. When I told her "no, thank you," she came unhinged. She thought I was acting smart, and told me so. I kept calm, and that got her madder and madder. We must have spent 10 minutes trying to solve the problem, and finally she got so red in the face I thought she'd blow up. She told me she'd see me after class.
>
> Maybe someone like me was a new thing for that teacher. But she wasn't new to me. I'd been through scenes like that all my life. You see, even though I'm 17 and a junior in high school, I can't read because I have dyslexia. I'm told I read "at a fourth-grade level," but from where I sit, that's not reading. You can't know what that means unless you've been there. It's not easy to tell how it feels when you can't read your homework assignments or the newspaper or a menu in a restaurant or even notes from your friends.
>
> —The New York Times, *25 April 1976, 12:15. Copyright © 1976 by The New York Times Company. Reprinted by permission.*

2. Here's the ending to David Raymond's essay. Notice how he purposely repeats the word *maybe* to drive home his point. Rewrite the ending of your dissonance essay, and try to do something similar to what Raymond has done in his conclusion.

> I've told this story because maybe some teacher will read it and go easy on a kid in the classroom who has what I've got. Or, maybe some parent will stop nagging his kid, and stop calling him lazy. Maybe he's not lazy or dumb. Maybe he just can't read and doesn't know what's wrong. Maybe he's scared, like I was.

3. Write the opening and closing for an essay on running away from home, getting caught cheating, losing a job, defying some authority, wrecking someone else's car, or a similar problem situation.

SET B: WRITING ACCURATELY

1. Sometimes you can get careless and lose track of the way a sentence is developing. You write the end of a sentence that doesn't match the one you began. The result is called a confused sentence or a mixed construction. Repunctuating will not correct this kind of error. You will have to rewrite the garbled passage into readable prose.

Confused: One reason to conclude her situation was hopeless would have to be related to her indecisive personality.
Revised: One reason for her hopeless situation is her indecisive personality.

Confused: If I decide to become a teacher doesn't mean it's too late to change later on.
Revised: If I decide to become a teacher, I can still change my mind later on.

Confused: By requiring drivers to have their cars checked periodically is one way to cut down on accidents.
Revised: Requiring drivers to have their cars checked periodically is one way to cut down on accidents.

Sentences can get confused in a number of ways. The only sure defense against sentence confusion is to understand the basic principles of sentence structure. Checking your writing carefully and reading your sentences aloud will also help.

Rewrite the following sentences to eliminate mixed and confused constructions.

a. By using a psychological approach to the story can provide important insights.
b. The changes of music are used in a way that the characters singing the jingle dance.
c. When waiting for a letter from home can be very frustrating.
d. In my high school, which is one of the best in the state, it's my feeling that it was much too easy.
e. By defining what "dissonance" means will be a good way to begin your essay.
f. After jogging six miles every day comes the time to take a hot shower and relax.
g. Even though you like a subject does not make it a good career choice.

2. Another kind of sentence confusion occurs whenever the subject and the rest of the sentence do not fit together. This problem is called *faulty predication* and arises when you carelessly complete a linking verb (is, am, are, was, were, will be, has been, becomes, appears, etc.) with a noun or an adjective that does not match the subject of the sentence. The result is a sentence that does not quite make sense. Consider this statement:

● Lyrics to country music are broken hearts and forgotten dreams.

The subject, *lyrics*, does not equal *broken hearts* and *forgotten dreams*; lyrics may be *about* such things or *include* them: the linking verb (*are*) sets up an equation that the sentence does not finish logically. Here are some other faulty predications followed by logical revisions:

Faulty: The importance of religion in the story is important to the main character's decision.
Logical: Religion is important to the main character's decision.

Faulty: The expression on their faces is usually pride.
Logical: The expression on their faces is usually a look of pride. (expression = look)

If you suspect a sentence of faulty predication, stripping it down to subject–verb–predicate noun or adjective can help you spot the problem. The faulty sentences just stated would look like this: Lyrics are hearts and dreams. Importance is important. Expression is pride.

Revise the following sentences to eliminate faulty predications.

a. The setting for the advertisement is a man and a woman walking through a jungle in Safari suits.
b. The actor's resonant voice was an outstanding performance.
c. Abortion is a national argument today.
d. The choice of Tommy as editor was chosen without regard for experience and ability.
e. Rock music is a negative attitude toward love and sex.

3. A frequent cause of faulty or awkward predication is the inaccurate use of *when* or *where* after a "being" verb—the "is when" or "is where" habit.

Mixed: One thing that keeps me from driving to the city is when I think of all the traffic.
Clear: One thing that keeps me from driving to the city is the thought of all the traffic. (thing = thought)

You will also want to avoid sentences that begin with "The reason" and continue with "is because." Common in speech, this construction is actually redundant, since *reason* means *because*.

Mixed: The reason their fuel bills are high is because they haven't insulated their attic.
Improved: Their fuel bills are high because they haven't insulated their attic.
Improved: The reason their fuel bills are high is that they haven't insulated their attic.

Revise the following sentences to eliminate the "is when" or "is where" usage and to clear up any "the reason...is because" constructions.

a. Flattery is when you compliment someone to obtain a favor.
b. The reason we chose this play is because it has a small cast.

c. Prejudice is when you make up your mind in advance of knowing the facts.
d. The reason we wanted to finish the chapter is because we were getting tired of putting the work off.
e. Where you make your mistake is capitalizing too many common nouns.

SET C: WRITING LOGICALLY AND COHERENTLY

1. Common sayings and popular expressions can be a source of dissonance. These sayings—also called *adages* or *maxims*—are repeated often because they're believed to contain wisdom and truth. Most of us have heard that "sticks and stones may break my bones, but words will never hurt me." Yet is this saying true? We all know that name-calling can hurt very much. Cruel names expose our weaknesses and jab us exactly where our skin is thinnest, and the popular maxim doesn't do much to soothe the sting of a sharp insult.

Write a three-paragraph essay about an adage like this one, and explain how you learned the truth behind the saying. In the first paragraph identify the adage, interpret it, if necessary, and give some background about your initial belief in its supposed wisdom. In the second paragraph tell how you came to discover that the saying was misleading or had oversimplified the truth. Finally, in the third paragraph draw some conclusion(s) about what you learned—about yourself, about other people, about believing in popular sayings.

The following are adages that you might have some thoughts on: use one of them or one of your own choosing for your brief essay.

- A winner never quits.
- Time heals all wounds.
- Love is blind.
- Nice guys finish last.
- The early bird gets the worm.
- He who hesitates is lost.
- Absence makes the heart grow fonder.
- It's not whether you win or lose, but how you play the game.

2. Many matters of public concern are controversial because there are strong arguments on both sides of the issue. It's not a sign of weakness or lack of commitment to admit that you can see more

than one side to a controversy—in fact, it may mean that you are thoughtful and well informed about the question. Write a paragraph in which you support the "other side" of a controversy. Here are some suggestions. You may modify the statements to fit your own views or construct your own concession to the other side of the debate.

a. I strongly oppose capital punishment, but I can understand why some people would want to execute serial killers.

b. Although beauty pageants are an insult to women, I can see why many young women find them attractive.

c. I sometimes think that student athletes should be paid for playing their sports.

d. Although I don't really believe that males are better suited for driving a car than females are, I think I know why people make fun of women drivers.

e. We shouldn't discriminate against the handicapped, but there may be times when employers are justified in refusing to consider a handicapped person for a job.

f. As a fan of boxing, I see why some people want to outlaw the sport.

g. Polygamy may be a good idea for some people.

h. Gun control has its drawbacks.

i. Video games may not be a complete waste of time and money.

3. In 1927 Walter Lippman wrote this defense of *stereotypes*:

> They are an ordered, more or less consistent picture of the world, to which our habits, our tastes, our capacities, our comforts, and our hopes have adjusted themselves. They may not be a complete picture of the world, but they are a picture of a possible world to which we are adapted. In that world, people and things have their well-known places, and do certain expected things. We feel at home there. We fit in. We are members. We know the way around. There we find the charm of the familiar, the normal, the dependable; its grooves and shapes are where we are accustomed to find them. And though we have abandoned much that might have tempted us before we creased ourselves into that mould, once we are firmly in, it fits as snugly as an old shoe.

> —*Walter Lippmann,* Public Opinion. *New York: Harcourt, 1927.*
> *Copyright © 1922, renewed 1950, by Walter Lippmann. New York:*
> *Macmillan Publishing Company.*

The *American Heritage Dictionary* defines a stereotype as "a person, group, event, or issue considered to typify or conform to an unvarying pattern or manner, lacking any individuality: *the very stereotype of a college sophomore.*" Think of a stereotype you once believed in—for instance, the absent-minded professor, the dumb jock, the cruel stepmother, the grouchy boss, the talkative barber. Why did you hold this stereotype? What happened to make you change your opinion? Write an essay that answers these questions.

CHAPTER SUMMARY

In this chapter you've studied

- organizing and developing an essay on dissonance
- evaluating the clarity and honesty of a classmate's paper
- using narrative openings
- employing purposeful repetition
- writing clear sentences
- reevaluating common sayings and stereotypes

13

IT'S ONLY ROCK 'N' ROLL: EXPRESSING OPINION

During its thirty-year history, rock music has been seen as both a positive and a negative influence on young people. In the 1950s Elvis Presley was branded wild and obscene, and many rock songs were attacked for their objectionable lyrics. In the late 1970s and the early 1980s, rock proved it could be a force for good, as musicians devoted time and money to help battle hunger around the world. In 1985 some parents' groups, alarmed at what they saw as a trend toward violent and sexually explicit lyrics, began to agitate for some kind of ratings on record albums, much like those for movies. So far, record companies have resisted actually rating records, saying they want to avoid acting as censors. The parents, however, claim censorship is not the issue. They say informing the public about the true nature of the lyrics is the point.

What do you think? The following article by a journalist surveys the debate for you. Here are brief definitions for some of the difficult words in the article:

VOCABULARY

| tumultuous | noisy and disorderly |
| vociferous | making an outcry |

unpalatable	unacceptable
decapitation	beheading
gyrating	rotating, twisting
alienated	made unfriendly
necrophilia	erotic attraction to corpses

ROCK'S WAR OF WORDS

Since its tumultuous birth in the 1950s, rock 'n' roll has provoked strong parental reaction. In 1954 outraged parents formed the Crusade for Decent Discs and lobbied radio stations to ban rock's "jungle" sounds as Elvis Presley's gyrating hips shocked television audiences. Now, three decades later, the crusade has come to life again. Prompted by the excesses of modern rock music and videos, Susan Baker, the mother of eight and wife of U.S. Treasury Secretary James Baker, formed the Parents Music Resource Center (PMRC) in Washington last May [1985]. Since then, her group has been waging a vociferous campaign to clean up what she calls "porn rock"—songs peppered with references to oral sex, incest, rape, sado-masochism and necrophilia. Last month [September 1985] a Senate committee tackled the subject of rock lyrics in a one-day hearing. And as a result of the ongoing campaign, 24 American record companies, representing 80 per cent of the record and tape business, have now agreed to issue warning labels on future offending albums.

But rock musicians are rebelling. Last week the newly formed Musical Majority, a group embracing several hundred musicians and industry executives, began organizing a counteroffensive. One group supporter, the eccentric rock performer Frank Zappa, whose own material often deals explicitly with sexual matters, dismissed labelling as "the equivalent of treating dandruff with decapitation." And for his part, Musical Majority founder Danny Goldberg, president of New York-based Gold Mountain Records, said he suspected that the parents' campaign was at least partly aimed at silencing unpalatable opinions of musicians. Said Goldberg: "Some political forces want to put music back in its place."

Many recording industry observers believe that the PMRC's powerful connections helped to exert pressure. With several other well-connected women, including Mary Elizabeth (Tipper) Gore, wife of Democratic Senator Albert Gore of Tennessee, Baker has monitored rock lyrics and found many of them to be pornographic. . . . High on the group's list of offenders is rock superstar Prince, whose song "Sister" includes lines such as "My sister never made love to anyone but me. . . ." The PMRC has also concluded that some songs by rock giants Bruce Springsteen, Cyndi Lauper and Michael Jackson are "unfit for children," but it reserves its greatest wrath for rock's "heavy metal" groups. The culprits it cites include Twisted Sister, Judas Priest and Mötley Crüe. . . .

At first, the declared aim of the parents' group was to force the recording industry to adopt a ratings system for offensive albums similar to movie classifications, without resorting to legislation. But in September the group did not object to the Recording Industry Association of America's compromise offer to try to regulate itself. Still, the prospect of having records labelled with stickers that say "Parental Guidance: Explicit Lyrics" alienated many members of the music industry. Appearing last month before the Senate Commerce Committee, Zappa found himself in an anti-labelling alliance with such diverse artists as country-pop balladeer John Denver and Twisted Sister's freakish lead singer, Dee Snider. . . .

Some industry observers like Goldberg said they believed that the labelling campaign has as much to do with politics as with sex or violence. This year's Live Aid and Farm Aid benefit concerts and recent campaigns against South Africa's apartheid were widely interpreted as signs of a new trend to politicization in rock music. But whatever the cause, some other industry insiders simply wish the controversy would die down. Said Brian Robertson, president of the Canadian Recording Industry Association: "The whole thing has mushroomed into a cause which is overblown."

—*Frances Kelly,* Maclean's, *14 October 1985, p. 95.*
Reprinted by permission of author.

KEY ESSAY

Where do you stand in the debate about rock and roll? Do you think rock songs refer too often to sex, drugs, and violence and have a bad influence on unsuspecting young people? Or do you agree with those who say that the negative impact of rock music has been exaggerated and that attempts to control the content of songs would threaten free speech? Make the strongest case you can for your position on these questions. Here are some guidelines:

1. Define your basic position clearly. Take a definite stand and explain it fully.
2. Try to break your main contention into particular points. Why is rock and roll so popular with young people? Where do young people get their values?
3. Give examples of specific works and performers who illustrate the excesses or benefits you are discussing.

QUESTIONS FOR ANALYZING WRITING

Read at least one opinion essay from a classmate. You might try to find a paper that opposes your own view. Answer each of the following questions in one or more sentences, and give your written responses to your classmate when you return the paper.

1. What do you see as the purpose of this essay?
2. To what specific readers do you think the essay is directed?
3. In which paragraph would you like to see more details, facts, examples? Why?
4. What details and examples strike you as particularly effective?
5. Does the author come across as caring about the issue? Quote important words that show concern (or lack of it).
6. Does the essay make you care about the subject? How?
7. Does the essay persuade you to agree with the writer's opinion? Why?

After returning the essay, look at the comments a classmate has written about your paper. Rewrite any parts that can be improved before you hand in the final draft of your essay.

EXERCISES

SET A: WRITING FLUENTLY

1. Ask someone you know how he or she feels about a controversial rock group or artist (like Prince, Judas Priest, Mötley Crüe, David Lee Roth, Twisted Sister, Shelia E., or Madonna). Then write a

long paragraph or two in which you both report the other person's opinion about the performer and express your own.

2. Write a one-page reaction to a specific song by a specific artist or group. Quote some key lines to help you express your opinion about the song. For instance, you might give your reactions to these lyrics by Mötley Crüe from "Too Young To Fall in Love":

> Well, now I'm killing you
> Watch your face turning blue.

3. In an article in *Newsweek* (12 August 1985) David Gates made this observation about women singers in the country music scene: "Female country singers once cultivated an image of purity, domesticity and humility. They wept in gratitude at awards shows, attributed their success equally to the Lord and their fans and never, never forgot their Tennessee mountain homes." Write a one-page comment about female singers in the rock or pop field. Who are they? Are they a lot alike? Are they as good as male singers? Why are there so many more male performers? Have female singers changed in the last few years?

SET B: WRITING ACCURATELY

1. When you write about your experiences and ideas, you use the pronoun *I* to identify yourself:

- *I* don't like the music of Van Halen.

When you want to address your readers directly (as we do in these instructions), you use the pronoun *you*:

- *You* need to listen carefully to the lyrics on Prince's latest album.

If you write about a person or persons, you usually mention the name first and then use *he*, *she*, or *they*:

- Some say Cyndi Lauper dresses the way *she* does in order to get media attention.

And if you refer to objects or ideas, you use *it* or *they* to talk about them:

- The lyrics on AC/DC's latest album are offensive because *they* seem to promote Satan worship.

The personal pronouns, then, represent three persons:

- First person—I, me, we, us
- Second person—you
- Third person—he, him, she, her, it, they, them

Unless you have a logical reason to shift, use the same person (we, you, they, I) consistently in your essay. The essay you read at the beginning of this chapter is written in the third person, with appropriate shifts from singular to plural.

In the following sentences, fill in the blanks with the personal pronouns that make the point of view consistent and sensible:

a. If a guitar player works hard, _____ has many chances for finding work, and _____ may even gain fame as well as financial reward.
b. I like Bruce Springsteen's songs because _____ treat subjects that relate to _____ and my life.
c. We want the industry to police itself. If _____ refuses, _____ are going to look into legal ways to stop what _____ feel is a form of contributing to the delinquency of minors.
d. Kids know what _____'re getting when _____ buy our records.
e. Listen to this song and then tell _____ if _____ think _____ is too explicit.

2. Rewrite the following sentences to eliminate incorrect shifts in person. (You may have to alter some verbs to make them agree with the pronouns you have changed.)

a. In high school I liked chemistry because it came easily to me, and the teacher let you progress at your own speed.
b. When I ask Roscoe for help with debugging a program, he never turns you down.
c. We are painfully aware that you can't count on the administration for support on touchy issues.
d. By the end of your first term as president, one feels that he is finally ready to do his job right.
e. Americans must vote for the people they want to run their government. We have no one else to blame if we get officials we don't want.
f. An artist should clean her brushes after each work session. Then you will find the brushes ready to use the next time you decide to paint.

3. Revise the following paragraph to make the point of view consistently *third person plural* (people/they):

> Most people are interested in music, either as a spectator or as performers. You can enjoy music by watching MTV or attending concerts. We can also enjoy playing records and listening to music on the radio. Other people want to make their own music. If we are really serious about playing an instrument or singing, we can take lessons and join a band or choir. You might prefer, however, to play for your own enjoyment or to entertain your friends and family at parties. A person has many chances to express his love of music.

SET C: WRITING LOGICALLY AND COHERENTLY

1. Consider these two viewpoints about censoring rock lyrics:

> I was in radio when we couldn't even use the word *cancer*. It was an absolute no-no. Nor could we ever say *syphilis*. What I'm saying is, if some of these four-letter words are prohibited, what's next?
>
> —*radio commentator Paul Harvey*

> Censorship should not be a bad word. No society can survive without it. I believe that the stop sign at the corner is healthy censorship. That's what the Constitution had in mind—self-imposed, majority-approved censorship.
>
> —*singer Pat Boone*

Write a page or so in which you defend or attack one of these quotations.

2. In September of 1985 *People Weekly* polled its readers about rock lyrics and asked these five questions:

- Do you believe explicit lyrics are harmful to children?
- Would you support a rating system for song lyrics?
- Would you support such a system for books and TV shows as well?
- Do you think that a rating system would lead to censorship?
- Should some lyrics be censored?

Using these questions to prod your own thinking, write a one-page position paper in which you state your opinion about a rating system for song lyrics.

3. Review the closing paragraph in your key essay. Write another conclusion in which you propose a way to reconcile the conflict about rock lyrics. Is there a way to balance the right of free speech with the right of parents to protect their children?

CHAPTER SUMMARY

In this chapter you've studied

- using examples to support an argument
- helping a fellow writer to be persuasive
- expressing controversial opinions
- using pronouns clearly
- avoiding shifts in person
- revising a conclusion

NO PASS, NO PLAY: LEARNING TO ARGUE

In 1983 the National Collegiate Athletic Association (NCAA) passed a new rule to toughen academic requirements for college athletes. The NCAA proposal, put into effect in 1986, requires that to win a scholarship and compete as a freshman, a high school senior must have a *C* average in a core curriculum (English, math, science, social science) and a minimum SAT score of 700. The proposal drew some strong criticisms, especially from those who felt it was really an attempt to reduce the dominance of blacks in college football and basketball. The following editorials present opposing positions on the NCAA rule. Read them and think about your own point of view on the NCAA decision and the issues it raises.

NEW RULE MAY PROVE HARMFUL

The National Collegiate Athletic Association has taken the initiative to tighten academic standards for prospective college freshmen in answer to the increasing concern among educators that athletes are being exploited. Effective in 1986, the new rule will require high school seniors to achieve a combined score of 700 on the Scholastic Aptitude Test before they are eligible for intercollegiate athletics.

While the NCAA's intent is honorable, its move to play the benevolent overseer may prove to be harmful to the student-athlete. Imposing minimum standards not only increases the barriers for minorities and educationally disadvantaged students, it shifts the focus from the root of the problem: the failure of universities and colleges themselves to take responsibility for the education of their athletes.

No doubt immediate action is called for. Only two percent of college athletes sign professional contracts in football, basketball or baseball. The remaining 98 percent too often are abandoned by the institutions that coddled them scholastically through four years of athletic performance. With a brief adieu the door slams. A worthless piece of parchment is too often the only tool for survival. . . .

The use of standardized tests to screen athletes is a negative and ill-conceived approach. Black educators who vehemently oppose the law may be justified in their belief that the tests are culturally biased. A 1981 study by the New York College Board reveals that approximately 56 percent of blacks scored below 700 while only 14 percent of whites scored below the cutoff. . . .

Gregory Anrig, president of the Educational Testing Service, which develops the SATs, praises the NCAA for having the courage to deal with the problem but feels there are "better and fairer ways" to accomplish those ends. "The idea of a cutoff is wrong. The SAT is not designed for a cutoff score. It's designed to be taken into consideration as one measure and not by itself," he said.

If measures taken by the NCAA are not fair, what is the solution? Ideally, colleges and universities should impose normal admissions standards on their athletes, then accept the responsibility of their scholastic progress.

To ensure that institutions are not exploiting their athletes, NCAA accrediting bodies should keep pressure on schools and take action when needed. Academic accrediting bodies should also monitor the way schools they review handle athletes; the central problem here is, after all, academic and not athletic.

The NCAA approach blames the victim, penalizing athletes whose talents are already exploited by colleges and universities.

Appropriate sanctions should be applied to the exploiters, through prohibitions against participation in NCAA supervised athletics. The choice is whether to penalize those who abuse the system, or as the NCAA has proposed, to penalize those who suffer its abuse.

— The Boston Globe, *28 January 1983. Reprinted courtesy of* The Boston Globe.

ATHLETES SHOULD BE STUDENTS TOO

It's regrettable that a new National Collegiate Athletic Association rule which toughens academic standards for athletes has been tagged with a "racist" label. . . .

Supporters of the rule view it as an effort to put pressure on secondary schools to prepare student athletes for a college life without basket-weaving courses.

Opponents contend, however, that the average scores for black students on SAT and ACT tests trail those of other students and therefore the tests contain a cultural bias.

Coaches of some of the nation's top college athletic powers are divided on the issue.

Coach Tom Osborne of the Nebraska Cornhuskers, who opposed the rule, considers the test discriminatory against students whose schools or family life did not encourage academic attainments or the majority culture's speech patterns.

Osborne says if the new requirements had been in force, one-third of the athletes currently in the Big Eight Conference would not have been allowed to compete as freshmen.

Joe Paterno, coach of the national gridiron champion Penn State, is on the other side of the argument. He charges that for 15 years black athletes have been "raped" by a system which exploits their talents without developing their minds. More and more black athletes are frustrated later in life because they didn't get what they should have gotten out of college. He predicted athletes will take up the challenge of meeting the new requirements.

We agree with those who contend the new rule will be a step toward reestablishing the integrity of institutions of higher learning, many of which have been wracked with athletic recruiting scandals. In all too many instances, "student" no longer applies in the term "student athletes."

It's time that something was done to correct the system which places a 17-year-old in an environment he is ill-prepared for. The NCAA is to be congratulated for reducing the chances that young men and women will be exploited for their athletic ability and then go unprepared to meet the challenges which will confront them when their playing days are over.

—Rapid City *[SD]* Journal, *20 January 1983.*

KEY ESSAY

As you read these editorials, you undoubtedly gathered that the argument about the NCAA rule raises a number of other issues: Do colleges and universities exploit athletes? Do standardized tests accurately measure the abilities of minority students? Are high schools adequately preparing their graduates for college? Decide what your answer is to one of these three questions, and develop your response into an essay of argument. Present your argument in the form of an editorial for your school or community newspaper. You may draw information from the two editorials above, but if you do, be sure to give proper credit for the facts and ideas you use.

The word *argument* sometimes means a heated disagreement that can lead to angry shouting and nasty threats. But an argument can be conducted in a calm, clear, reasonable manner. When you write an essay in which you try to get someone (like a teacher) to agree with what you're saying, you are writing an essay of argument. To get your reader's agreement, you will have to write clearly, carefully, and convincingly. The following explanation will help you understand how to make a convincing argument in writing.

ELEMENTS OF ARGUMENT

The basic components of a good argument have been described by philosopher Stephen Toulmin as the *claim*, the *evidence*, and the *warrant*. According to Toulmin, these elements are always present in an argument, whether they are stated or not. When you argue, you make claims, support them with evidence, and explain or assume some connection between the claim and the evidence. This connection is called the *warrant*, and it is often the most important element in a persuasive argument. (One of the dictionary definitions of "warrant" is "justification"; think of the term in this sense rather than in the sense of "guarantee" or "arrest papers.")

Here is a simple example. You look at the sky and say that it's going to rain because you see dark clouds rolling in. Your claim is that it's going to rain, and your evidence comes from the dark clouds you see. The warrant is that dark clouds usually mean rain, but you didn't state that connection because you probably expected that your listeners would understand and share your judgment.

The warrant is important because it holds the argument together. It's an assumption that stands behind the argument and links the evidence to the claim. When someone disagrees with you, it is often because he or she does not accept the warrant for your claim. For instance, people who don't share the belief that dark clouds usually mean rain may well reject your argument that it's going to rain because you see dark clouds in the sky. These people aren't denying the evidence—they can see the dark clouds; they just don't share your assumption about what such clouds mean.

THE IMPORTANCE OF WARRANT

Let's look at another simple argument to illustrate the importance of the warrant. Hector claims that Ty Cobb is the best hitter in the history of baseball. His evidence is that Cobb had a lifetime batting average of .367. Rosalie disagrees. She says that Hank Aaron is the best hitter in baseball and supports her claim with this evidence: Aaron had more total home runs, more extra-base hits, and more runs batted in than any other player. Hector and Rosalie both have accurate evidence, but they make different assumptions about it. Hector assumes that lifetime batting average is the best way to rank hitters, while Rosalie assumes that her standards are the ones to use in ranking the all-time hitters. If these two baseball fans were to ask you to decide which one of them is right, what could you say? Well, if you want to stick strictly to the terms of the argument, you would have to choose between the warrants: you would have to decide which of the two assumptions about criteria for judging hitters was the better one. It's possible, of course, to say that both warrants are valid, but that wouldn't resolve the dispute. You would, however, have identified the true source of the disagreement by sorting out the warrant from the other two components (claim and evidence) and focusing on that element.

When you write your essay, take the time to analyze your arguments carefully. Do you always state the connection between your claims and your evidence? Are your warrants likely to be challenged? Do you need to anticipate such challenges and offer some explanations or backing for your warrants?

QUESTIONS FOR ANALYZING WRITING

Read a classmate's argument essay. Then, respond in writing to the following questions:

1. Identify the major claims in the essay's argument and evaluate the evidence for each one. Which claims have adequate support? Which claim or claims need more support?
2. Where has the writer made the connections between claims and evidence clear? Are there any assumptions that have not been stated? Indicate what they are and state what you think the unstated assumptions are.
3. Would you challenge any of the warrants? Briefly explain your objections.
4. Is the argument clear and convincing? Point out any weak or unclear parts.

EXERCISES

SET A: WRITING FLUENTLY

1. Interview some people about the NCAA rule on admission standards for athletes. Talk to a coach, a student-athlete, another professor, and a non-athlete student. Write a brief paper in which you use the opinions of these people to illustrate what the main issues in the controversy are.

SET B: WRITING ACCURATELY

1. Learning to see your mistakes—and to correct them—is an important part of becoming a good editor and a good writer. In the following passage, correct as many errors as you can find. About fifty changes are needed.

"Final exams take all the joy out of my life, moaned Bumper. "School wouldnt be half bad if we didnt have to take tests."

"Yeah. I think Id rather take an exam then write a paper," responded Clint. Its easier to memorize then to think—an you have to think too be able to write good."

If they'd just be reasonable, we wouldn't have to do either."

"But we probable wouldn't learn to much if we didnt take tests would we?"

Bumper slapped his forhead and groaned. Than he ask Clint, "Do you believe everything they tell you? Its nothing but propaganda. They're only prupose in giving exams is to decide whom gets what grade."

Clint was quite for a few minutes as he leafed thru the world history text spred out in front of him. "If you want my advise, Id say youd better quite complaining and start studying because your going to have to take that exam tomorrow weather you like it or not."

"Good grief, ever time I try to get some sympathy out of you, I get a lecture instead. Who's side are you on, anyway?"

"Im not on anybodies side. I just think we ought to quite wasteing time. Have you considered how it will effect you're life if you flunk you're final," asked Clint with an edge of impatience in his voice.

You've got me their, old buddy," admitted Bumper sadly. "Id probable have to go to summer school to try to rise my grade point average. I'll just get myself one more cup of coffee than I'll set down and really hit these books"

SET C: WRITING LOGICALLY AND COHERENTLY

1. A friend of yours makes the claim that professional wrestling is a stupid waste of time. The evidence he ves comes from an article which says that 90% of the action i d. What warrant connects evidence to his claim? Can you cha nge the warrant? Write an argument that makes another claim (or claims) based on the evidence. Make your argument clear by fully explaining how you connect the evidence to your conclusion(s).

2. The following paragraph is taken from an article by Norman Ellenberger, a former head basketball coach at the University of New Mexico who was convicted of twenty-one counts of fraud for

altering academic transcripts of athletes. Analyze Ellenberger's arguments: What assumptions does he make about student athletes? Do you agree with these assumptions? Write your response to Ellenberger's claims. Do not address your arguments to Ellenberger himself, but write to someone (like a classmate) who has read this article and seems to agree with its viewpoint.

> Who cares whether [the disadvantaged student-athlete] graduates from college? It is not that important. He did not want to go to college in the first place. He is performing a service. He is doing what he is supposed to do. That does not make him a bad person. And when he is through, sure, we would like to graduate him, but we can't. There is no program in any university that he can handle. But he is one hell of an athlete. He can run up and down the basketball court for you. He will bring you money. He will do all these things that people say are so dastardly. But don't you know that that young man is benefiting, that he is learning to be a person, that he is developing, that he is becoming a member of society? Some of the greatest young men whom I have ever been fortunate to coach never graduated. But they have jobs, they have families, and they are not in the breadlines. The reason: they came and put on a pair of short pants and sneakers and ran up and down the basketball court.

> —*Normal Ellenberger, "Tell It Like It Is: We Have to Make Money,"* from The Center Magazine, *January/February 1982. Reprinted with permission from* The Center Magazine, *a publication of The Center for the Study of Democratic Institutions.*

CHAPTER SUMMARY

In this chapter you've studied

- using the three basic elements of an argument
- writing an editorial
- analyzing other writers' arguments
- synthesizing the issues in a controversy
- proofreading a passage
- responding to an argument

15

THE "YOU ATTITUDE": APPLYING FOR A JOB

Probably one of the most important things you will ever write is a job application letter. What counts most in this writing task is clarity and content—and a clever way of conveying your information that business writing specialists call the "YOU attitude."

The "YOU attitude" is easy to explain but not so easy to achieve. It involves remembering to focus on *you* (the prospective employer) as well as on *I* (the writer/applicant). It also involves being complimentary, but unless you stop short of flattery, your letter will sound insincere. A good job application letter is tough to write. You'll do well to start practicing now. When the time comes to compose the real letter, it may be the most important single page you'll ever write. Here are some pointers.

1. Decide what you want to say before you write.
2. Decide the best way to order your material.
3. Be concise and selective: your resume (see Figure 15–3) will provide additional details.
4. Address your letter to someone by name, if possible; otherwise, begin with "Dear Director of Personnel."
5. Be polite and straightforward: don't be flowery or familiar.

```
                                        1527 Kingsridge Road
                                        Lexington, IL 61708
                                        March 10, 1985


     Director of Personnel
     State Farm Insurance Company
     One State Farm Plaza
     Bloomington, IL  61701

     Dear Personnel Director:

          Because I believe your firm offers the widest
     opportunity for professional growth in my field of any
     insurance company in this area, I am applying to State Farm.
     At the end of April I will complete my bachelor's degree in
     Applied Computer Science at the Illinois Technological
     University.

          During the fall semester of my senior year I served an
     internship in the Agency Systems Division of Country Companies
     Insurance.  I worked with microcomputer systems, mainly on
     property/casualty applications.  A list of my major
     assignments during that internship follows:
               --Technical design, coding and testing of Individual
                 Health Rate Quotes;
               --Testing for a sales letter system on an IBM 8100
                 network;
               --Design and programming for CC Communications, a
                 package that allows IBM PCs to communicate with IBM
                 mainframes.

          During my internship at Country Companies, I worked with
     Mr. James Snyder and Ms. Judith Ivey, both of whom have agreed
     to serve as references.  You might also wish to contact Dr.
     Larry Eggan and Dr. Jan Cook, who were my professors at
     Illinois Tech.  Addresses and telephone numbers for these
     people appear on my resume.

          If you have need of someone with my training, I will be
     pleased to come in for an interview at your convenience.  I
     would certainly like to be associated with a nationally-known
     company like State Farm.  Thanks for your consideration.

                                    Yours sincerely,

                                    Michele Finley
                                    Michele Finley
```

Figure 15-1 Job Application Letter

6. Use the serious tone and formal English that you studied in Chapter 9.
7. Use a standard business letter format (see Figure 15-1).
8. Use standard English—the conventions of punctuation and usage we've been explaining.
9. Revise your letter at least three times—more, if needed.

10. Use bond paper and type neatly—or better yet, hire a professional typist.
11. Proofread carefully: CORRECTNESS COUNTS!

Figure 15–1 shows you a job application letter that follows this advice. Notice, it's only one page long, centered vertically and horizontally, and single-spaced with generous margins. About the writer, it includes only the important information that would interest this employer. It sneaks in the "YOU attitude," focusing on the prospective employer in the first and last paragraphs. It is written in formal standard English, is correctly punctuated, and contains no careless errors. It also illustrates the most commonly used format for a business letter.

KEY ESSAY

The letter that appears in Figure 15–2 ignores virtually every one of the pointers provided at the beginning of this chapter. The format—except for the "To Whom It May Concern" part—is correct. You may follow this format instead of the one used in Figure 15–1, if you prefer.

Your job now is to revise this letter until you produce a version that would be guaranteed to get you an interview. Look over the sample letter in Figure 15–1 and study the pointers at the beginning of this chapter before you begin.

QUESTIONS FOR ANALYZING WRITING

Trade revised letters with a classmate. Read the page carefully and then write on a separate sheet of paper your responses to these questions.

1. List the major improvements that the writer has made.
2. Does the writer need to add information? Or perhaps take some out? If so, what? Make specific suggestions.
3. Is the material effectively arranged? Should any of the information be moved?
4. Is the language suitable? Too chatty and familiar? Too stilted?

```
800 West Main St.
Normal, IL  61761
December 23, 1986


The Pet Supply Center
226 North College Ave.
Bloomington, IL  61701

To Whom It May Concern;

I read your ad in the paper and see that you are looking for a
Manager for your Store.  As luck would have it, I'm looking
for a better job because the one I have doesn't pay very
good.  I've worked here six months.

As you can see from my enclosed resume, I have had a variety
of job experiences.  I've worked as a Certified Nurses
Assistent in three different nursing homes working my way
through college.  Getting an accounting job in this town is
pretty hard.  But I've lived all my life here and want to stay
here, so I'd be a steady employe.

I'm working as assistant Manager at this resterant but I could
do a better job than he does.  I get along better with the
customers and thother people who work here.  So I think I
could Manage your Pet Supply Store without any trouble.

I had a Boxer dog when I was growing up and we have a cat but
I'm sure I could learn about other animals too.

Please call me for an interview on either Friday or Saturday
of this week as they are my day's off and I don't know what my
schdule for next week is yet.

Yours truely,

Arnold Smedley

Arnold Smedley
```

Figure 15–2   Letter to Revise

Suggest words that need changing. What words strike you as particularly well chosen?

5. Has the writer achieved the "YOU attitude"? If not, how could it be accomplished?

6. Are there errors in grammar, punctuation, or spelling? Any typos? Point these out by paragraph and line number.

When you get your paper back, consider your editor's suggestions, and revise your letter until you consider it flawless.

EXERCISES

SET A: WRITING FLUENTLY

1. As you probably guessed, now it's time to write your own job application letter. You can include your own experience and qualifications, or you can make up a set you wish you had. Pattern your letter on the example in Figure 15–1: make this an application for your first job following graduation, and make it a "feeler" letter (not in response to a specific job advertisement, but an inquiry to see if perhaps there is an opening). Begin by reviewing the pointers given at the beginning of this chapter.

2. Now you need to put together a resume to go with that letter of application that you just wrote. Look at the sample resume in Figure 15–3 and notice these things about it:

a. List your job experiences from the most recent to your first job. Include everything—from babysitting to mowing lawns to volunteer work to working at McDonald's. If listing everything will make your resume run to two pages, though, cut out low-level or irrelevant jobs in the distant past.

b. List your education the same way—most recent first—and include your overall grade point average, if it's respectable.

c. Make a heading for "Honors and Awards," if you have any. It's fine to include even popularity awards, like "Most Popular Senior," because these reflect your personality. Don't forget offices held.

d. When you do a resume to actually send out, remember that you need to get permission from your references before giving their names, addresses, and telephone numbers.

e. Unless you're a whiz at the word processor, you need to get your resume professionally typed. NEATNESS COUNTS! It can be done on ordinary paper, though, and photocopied.

f. Proofread carefully. CORRECTNESS COUNTS!

Now, write your resume and make it look as attractive as possible by using a consistent format and plenty of white space.

3. Look through the classified ads in your local newspaper and find one that appeals to you. Write a letter applying for that specific

RESUME

Michele Finley
1527 Kingsridge, Lexington, IL 61708
Ph. 309-453-5697

Work Experience

Aug.-Dec.   Student Intern, Country Companies Insurance
   1985   Bloomington, IL

Aug.-May   Undergraduate Teaching Assistant, Computer
  1984-85   Science Department, Illinois Technological U.

June 1982-   Cashier, Crown Theater (part-time)
Aug. 1984   Lexington, IL

June-Aug. 1981   Dairy Queen, counter attendant, Lexington, IL

Education

Aug. 1982-   Illinois Technological University
  Present
May 1985   Will receive B.S. in Applied Computer Science
                    Expected Grade Point Average: 3.1 (on 4.0 scale)

June 1982   Graduated from Lexington High School,
                    Lexington, IL GPA: 3.87 (on 4.0 scale)

Honors

Outstanding ACS senior, Illinois Tech, 1985
President of the Illinois Tech Computer Club, 1983-84
Graduated cum laude from Lexington High School

References

Dr. Jan Cook   Dr. Larry Eggan   Mr. James Snyder   Ms. Judith Ivey
ACS Dept.   Chair, ACS Dept.   Country Companies   Country Companies
Illinois Tech.   Illinois Tech.   IAA Drive   IAA Drive
Fox, IL 61706   Fox, IL 61706   Normal, IL 61761   Normal, IL 61761
309/438-7217   309/438-7275   309/688-3342   309/688-3464

Figure 15–3   Resume

job. Feel free to manufacture for yourself any qualifications that seem suitable.

Don't mail the letter. Instead, exchange with a classmate, read each other's letter, and decide whether you would agree to interview the applicant. If you decide not to, be prepared to explain what about the letter put you off.

SET B: WRITING ACCURATELY

1. Because you need to be extra careful about correctness when you write a letter applying for a job, you may need to review the main principles for capitalization. You know, of course, always to capitalize the first letter of each sentence and the pronoun *I*. You also capitalize the names of specific persons and things, as well as titles:

- I think Mr. Johnson is the personnel manager.
- Dear Personnel Manager: (used as if a person's name)

- Wow, what a tall building!
- Yes, that's the Empire State Building.

- Clyde Crashcup was recently promoted to captain.
- That's Captain Crashcup's desk over there.

Now, reread the bad example of a job application letter in Figure 15–2. What errors in the use of capital letters do you find? Rewrite each word that needs the capitalization corrected.

2. Abbreviations are acceptable on your resume where space is at a premium (*Dept.* for Department, *IL* for Illinois), but you must be consistent. If you use *IL* the first time, don't accidentally switch to *Ill.* the next time you shorten the name.

Also, some terms are almost always abbreviated—like titles used before names (Dr., Ms., Mr., Mrs.); degrees (Ph.D., D.V.M., R.N., M.D.); and some organizations (UNESCO, YMCA, IBM). But write out the titles of organizations the first time you use them; then, abbreviate them after that.

Notice that if a title is used without a person's name, it must be written out:

- The doctor is in, but you will still have to wait.
- Dr. Dolores Dearheart often makes house calls.
- Dolores Dearheart, M.D., was called as a witness.
- Mr. Thomas Tuttle has become a registered nurse.
- You should hire Tom Tuttle, R.N., if you need help.

The following sentences, written in formal language, contain improper abbreviations. Rewrite to correct the mistakes.

a. Arnold plans to become a medical dr. like his mother.
b. By going to Doctor Dimwit, one may save $.

c. The supt. needs the st. address of each applicant.
d. In what dept. does one pay a parking ticket?
e. One must fill in a form & write out a check.

3. Most people know to underline in order to indicate italics. But do you remember *when* you're supposed to italicize? Here are some guidelines for using italics and quotation marks:

- Underline the titles of written works that are long, like books, plays, movies, and book-length poems.
- Put quotation marks around titles of short works, like stories, chapters, poems, and one-act plays.
- Never underline or put in quotation marks the title of your own written work (unless the title *is* a quotation).
- Underline or put in quotation marks words used as words (You have too many *and*s in this sentence).
- Underline foreign words if your dictionary shows them in italics.

Copy the following paragraph, adding underlining or quotation marks where needed. Consult your dictionary, if in doubt.

> If you've only read The Scarlet Letter and the short story, Ethan Brand, you shouldn't act as if you've studied Hawthorne's entire work. And you mustn't be so cavalier about acknowledging your library sources. If a critic discusses Hawthorne's tragic vision and you borrow that phrase, you must indicate that it is not your own by putting the phrase in quotation marks. Also notice that you've spelled Hawthorne without the e, and you've repeated the word indeed five times.

SET C: WRITING LOGICALLY AND COHERENTLY

1. If, after applying for a job, you've had an interview in which everything went well, you want to be sure the person who interviewed you keeps you in mind for the position. The best way to do this is to write a follow-up letter in which you *briefly* thank the person for considering you for the job. You might mention—if you can do so without sounding insincere—something about the firm or its management that you admired. But be careful: you must pay a graceful compliment without fawning or gushing.

Now, imagine that you have just enjoyed a successful interview for the job you applied for as manager of a pet store. Write a short "thank you for the interview" letter. Remember that correctness counts just as heavily in this note as it did in the letter of application. And you still must follow faithfully a standard business letter format.

2. Sooner or later, you'll probably need to write a business letter requesting something or complaining about something. Your results will probably be better if you know how to write an effective letter. Here are some suggestions:

- Explain clearly what you need or what went wrong.
- Provide necessary order numbers or model numbers.
- If complaining, suggest what you think should be done to ensure your satisfaction.
- If requesting something, enclose a stamped, self-addressed envelope.
- Be polite, reasonable, and confident that your merchandise will be repaired or your money refunded.
- Close with a word of thanks for expected help.
- Follow a standard business letter format.
- Be sure your letter is error-free.

The letter of complaint in Figure 15–4 falls short of following these guidelines. Revise it until you consider it an effective letter.

3. If your social life is to match the success of your business career, you must face up to the obligation to write thank-you notes for gifts and favors received from family and friends. You should also write notes of congratulations to friends and colleagues who receive honors or earn promotions. Good manners require these brief acknowledgments, and they are not a bit hard to write once you get the hang of it.

First, get some tasteful notecards. They can either be plain or say something simple, like "Thank you," on the front. The advantage of using cards is that you are thus relieved of the need to cover a whole page of paper with writing. You can't wedge more than a few sentences inside one of those little cards, thank goodness.

You can write as informally as you like, but you are still obliged to be sincere. Simply thank the reader for the gift or the kindness, mentioning what it is by name that you are grateful for. Try, if possible, to say how much you're going to enjoy having, wearing, or

```
Feb. 10th


Not-So-Dear Gas Company;
     I don't have gas heat, but my bill was still more then
my friend's, an she does have gas heat, which I think is
pretty outrageous, even if I do have a gas dryer.
     Last month my bill seemed high, but I didn't say
anything because I know you never give anyone the chance to
prove you're wrong.  This month, tho, I just couldn't believe
how far off the bill was from what it should be, and so I
decided to write anyways even tho it won't do any good.
     If you had any sense of responsibility, you would check
my gas bill or try to find out what went wrong with my meter,
but I'm sure you're much too busy counting your profits to do
right by a customer.
Heatedly yours,


G. Hamilton
1210 Greengables Rd.
Bloomington, Ill.  61701
```

Figure 15–4   Second Letter to Revise

using the present, or how much the kindness means to you. Conclude with "Sincerely" or "With love," depending upon your closeness to the reader. Respond promptly and write legibly (such personal messages should not be typed).

Now, write a polite note to your instructor in this course thanking her or him for helping you to improve your writing. Or, if you owe someone a long-overdue thank-you note, by all means, write that instead.

CHAPTER SUMMARY

In this chapter you've studied

- writing a job application letter
- employing the "YOU attitude"
- compiling a resume
- writing a follow-up letter
- writing a letter of request
- writing a letter of complaint
- writing a letter of thanks
- using capital letters
- using abbreviations
- using underlining and quotation marks